The Question Challenge®

Card Game Fun Sheets

A Companion Book for the Question Challenge™ Card Game

**by Kim A. Gill, M.A., CCC-SLP and
Joanne P. DeNinno, M.S., CCC-SLP
Edited by Julie A. Daymut, M.A., CCC-SLP and Erin Riojas**

Printed in the United States

ISBN 978-1-60723-023-6

Super Duper® Publications
www.superduperinc.com
Post Office Box 24997 • Greenville, SC 29616 USA
1-800-277-8737 • Fax 1-800-978-7379

Introduction

The Question Challenge™ Card Game Fun Sheets reinforces students' expressive and receptive language skills in 10 areas that are necessary for effective communication and problem solving.

- Inferencing
- Understanding Sarcasm
- Determining Perspective
- Staying Calm Through Self-Talk
- Stating Opinions
- Predicting
- Intonation & Body Language
- Cognitive Flexibility
- Social Encouragement
- Questioning in Conversation

This book complements *The Question Challenge™ Card Game* published by Super Duper® Publications. *The Question Challenge™ Card Game Fun Sheets* uses the same prompts and photos found in the game and displays them in a worksheet format. The activity sheets are great for homework or therapy use.

The activity pages are designed for students in grades 1–12. By completing these sheets, students improve their reasoning and social skills, such as taking another person's perspective, turn-taking, and interpreting body language. Each page also builds vocabulary skills and encourages following directions.

The pages provide a variety of activities, including matching games, word searches, crossword puzzles, game boards, cube rolls, word associations, memory games, story-writing activities, drawing activities, and more. There is also an answer key! Print any of the workbook pages in black and white or full color using the included CD-ROM.

Contents

Contents

Dear Parent/Helper,

_________________________ is currently learning about expressive and receptive language skills.
(Child's Name)

Today your child learned about ____.
(Skill)

The attached worksheet will help your child practice and reinforce this skill. Your child will bring home more of these worksheets throughout the year.

☐ After you review the worksheet with your child, please sign and return the page by

_________________________.
(Date)

☐ Please review the worksheet with your child. You do not need to return the page.

☐ ____

____

____

Thank you for your support!

____
Teacher/SLP Signature

____
Date

____
Parent/Helper Signature

____
Date

Inferencing – Match It Up

Instructions: Read each situation and answer the question that goes with it. Under each photo write the number of the situation that matches it. Then circle the words in the sentences that gave you clues.

A. [ ] B. [ ] C. [ ] D. [ ]

E. [ ] F. [ ] G. [ ] H. [ ]

1. Johnny watched the player dribble down the court and sink a three-point shot. *Where was Johnny?*

2. The colorful leaves covered the ground. *What time of year was it?*

3. Julie went up the escalator, past the food court, to the department store. *Where was she?*

4. The woman in the black robe called for order in the court. *What was her job?*

5. Sam logged in and typed a message to his friend. *What was he doing?*

6. Sara grabbed her black bag with her stethoscope and thermometer. *What was Sara's job?*

7. We dressed in red, white, and blue clothes and watched the fireworks display. *What time of year was it?*

8. John went to the library, did research, and began to write. *What was John doing?*

Name   Date   Helper

Inferencing – Memory Game

Instructions: Cut out the cards. Shuffle and place all cards facedown. Player One chooses two cards to try to match the situation card with the corresponding inference card. Player Two follows in turn. The player with the most matches wins.

Tommy took his medicine and crawled into bed.	 He was sick.	We dressed in red, white, and blue clothes and watched the fireworks display.	 It was the Fourth of July.
The scientist looked through the eyepiece and viewed the bacteria on the slide.	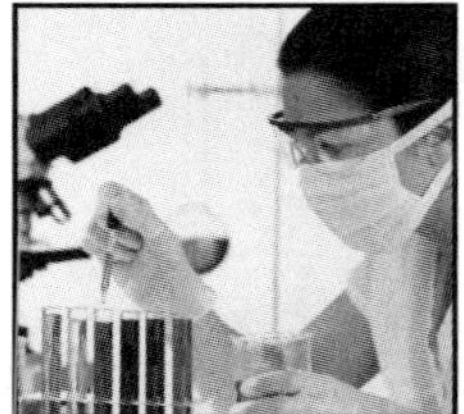 She was looking through a microscope.	You left the windows open at your house, and it started raining.	 The rain will come in the windows.
When we were lost, we looked at the needle on this to find our way.	 We used a compass.	You took your new notebooks and backpack with you on your first day.	 You were going to school.
Joey read 150 books and won first prize in the fourth grade reading contest.	 Joey read the most books.	The circus clown tossed the brightly colored balls into the air without dropping any.	 He was juggling.

_________________________ _________________________ _________________________
Name   Date   Helper

Inferencing – Where Was the Photo Taken?

Instructions: Read each situation and find the photo on the map that matches it. Then write the name of the city where the photo was taken. Tell what is going on in each situation.

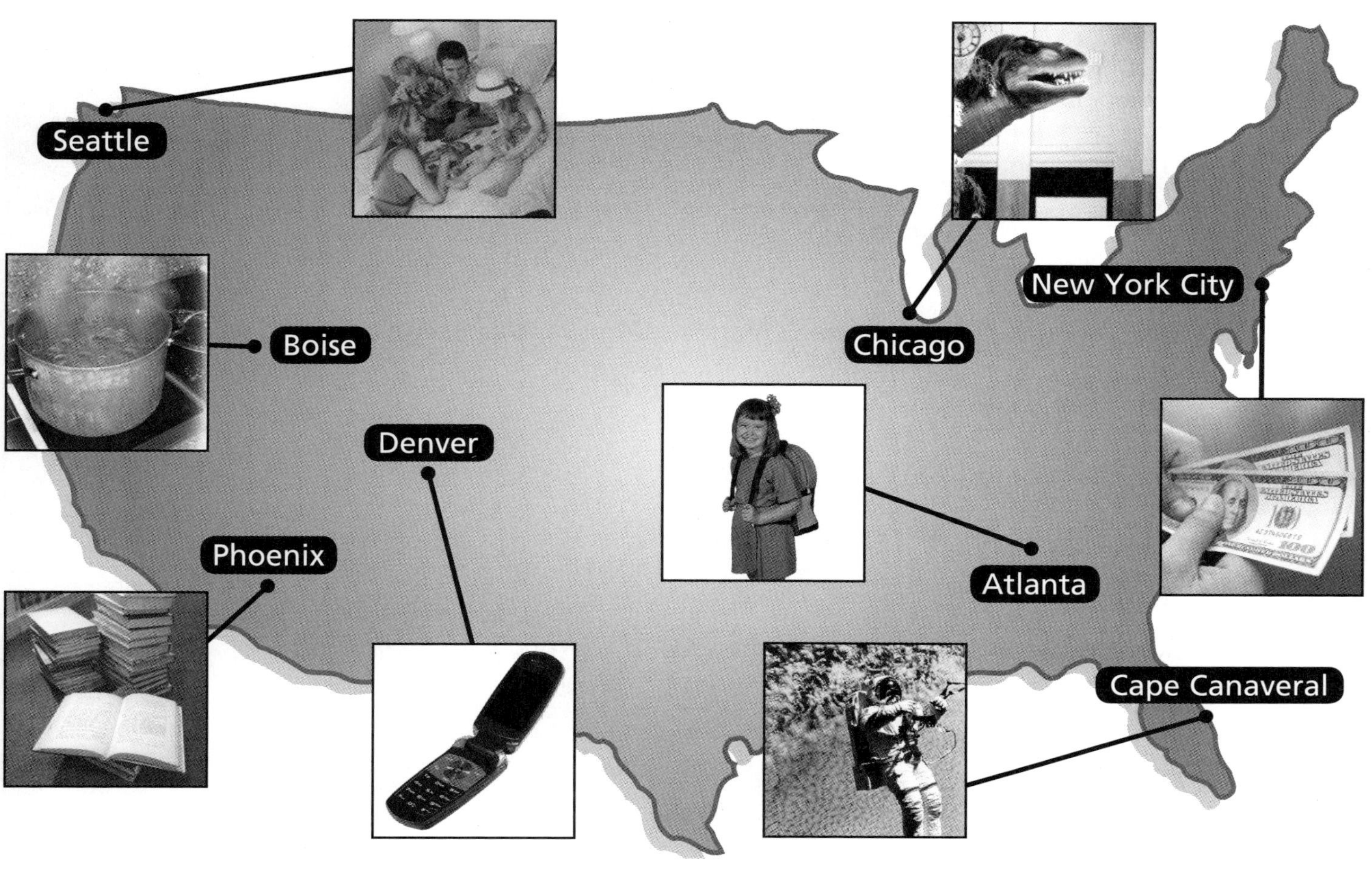

1. We love the dinosaur and the African animal exhibits. City – _______________________________________

2. We climbed in the shuttle and waited for the countdown. City – _______________________________________

3. We checked in and got our room keys. City – _______________________________________

4. The teller counted the money and put it in the vault. City – _______________________________________

5. You took your new notebooks and backpack with you on your first day. City – _______________________

6. You tried to call your dad on your cell phone, but it would not turn on. City – _______________________

7. Mom was boiling water on the stove and was distracted by the baby crying. City – _______________

8. John went to the library, did research, and began to write. City – _______________________________________

_______________________________________   _______________   _______________________________________
Name   Date   Helper

Inferencing – The Best Inference

Instructions: Read each situation and the question that goes with it. Then circle the best inference that goes with the situation.

1. Sam logged in and typed a message to his friend. *What was he doing?*

   A. Sam was emailing.

   B. Sam was printing an essay.

   C. Sam was doing online research.

2. The baby was playing with a bag of small marbles. *Why was this a problem?*

   A. The baby might have lost the marbles.

   B. The baby could have choked.

   C. The marbles belonged to the baby's older brother.

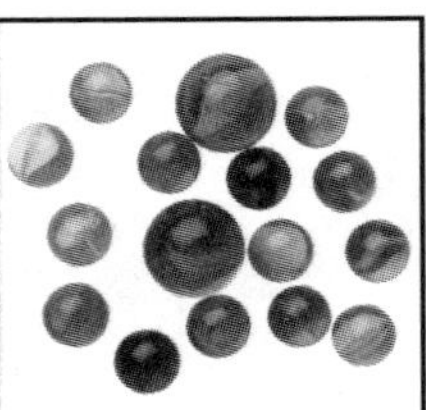

3. Tommy took his medicine and crawled into bed. *What is wrong with Tommy?*

   A. Tommy is thirsty.

   B. Tommy is sad.

   C. Tommy is sick.

4. Johnny watched the player dribble down the court and sink a three-point shot. *Where was Johnny?*

   A. Johnny was at a hockey game.

   B. Johnny was at a basketball game.

   C. Johnny was behind the school.

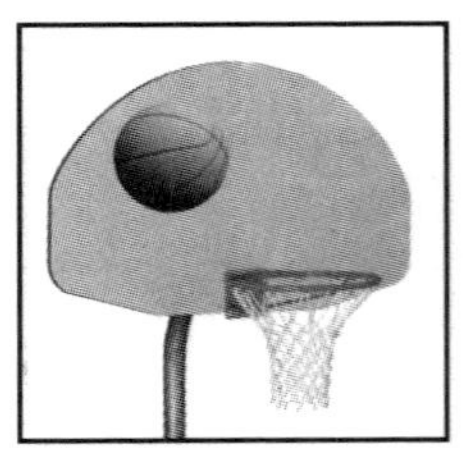

5. Joey read 150 books and won first prize in the fourth grade reading contest. *Why did Joey win?*

   A. Joey finished the competition before anyone else.

   B. Joey liked to read.

   C. Joey read the most books.

Name	Date	Helper

Inferencing – Answer It

Instructions: To assemble the cube, cut on the dotted lines. Fold on the solid lines and glue/tape as indicated. To play, roll the cube. Read the situation on the top side of the cube and answer the question.

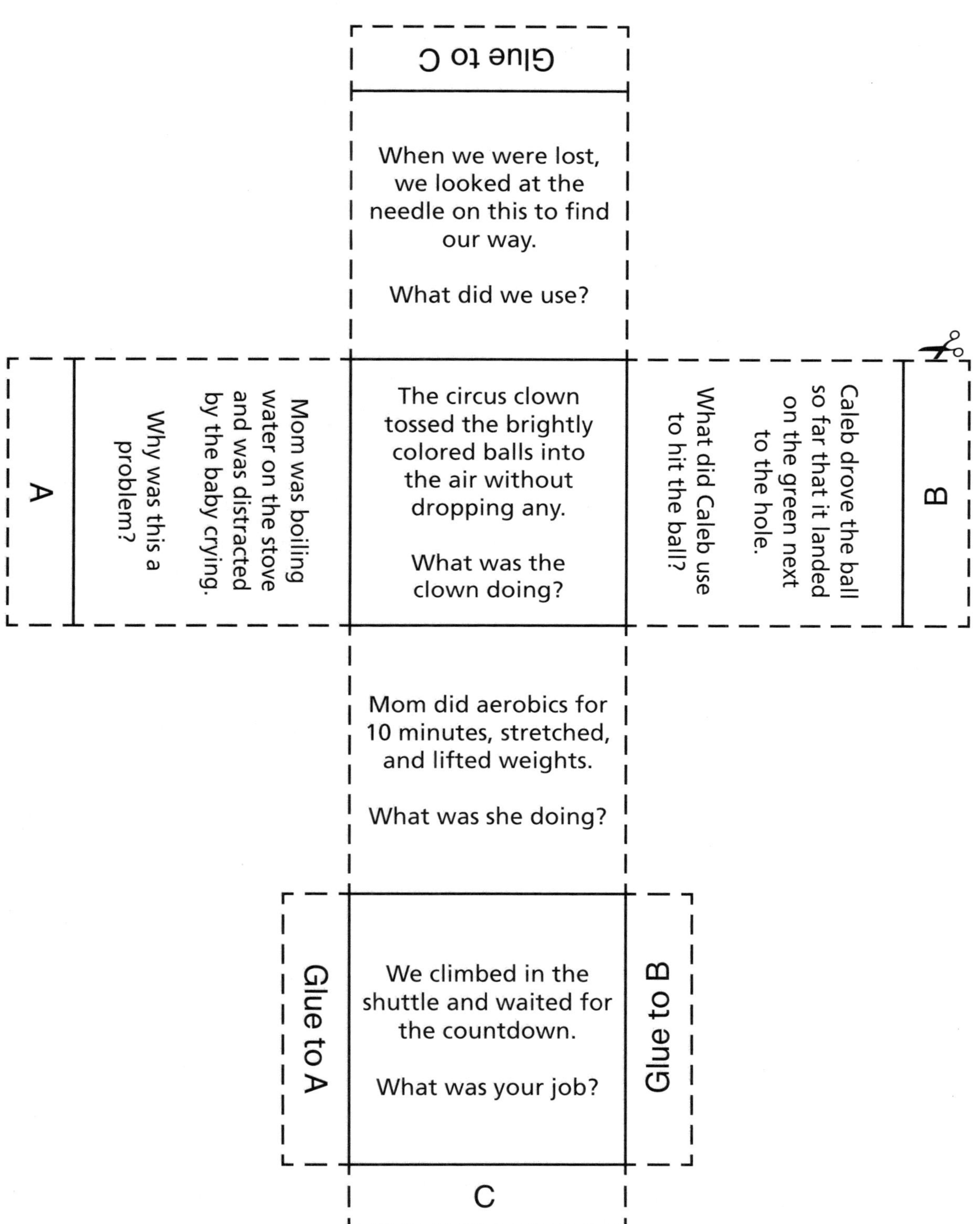

______________________   ______________________   ______________________
Name   Date   Helper

Inferencing – What Do You Need?

Instructions: Cut out the photos at the bottom of the page. Then glue/tape each photo next to the situation that goes with it.

1. Nicole wanted to see the bird up close.

4. It was the first day of school.

2. Tommy was sick.

5. We were in the Fourth of July parade.

3. It started raining.

6. We were lost on our hike.

Name   Date   Helper

Inferencing – Act It Out

Instructions: Cut out the cards. Shuffle and place all cards facedown. Player One chooses a card and acts out the scene on the card. Other players try to guess what Player One is doing. Play continues in turn.

Act like you are sick.

Act like you are playing golf.

Act like you are looking through binoculars.

Act like your cell phone is broken.

Act like you are a clown.

Act like you are doing aerobics.

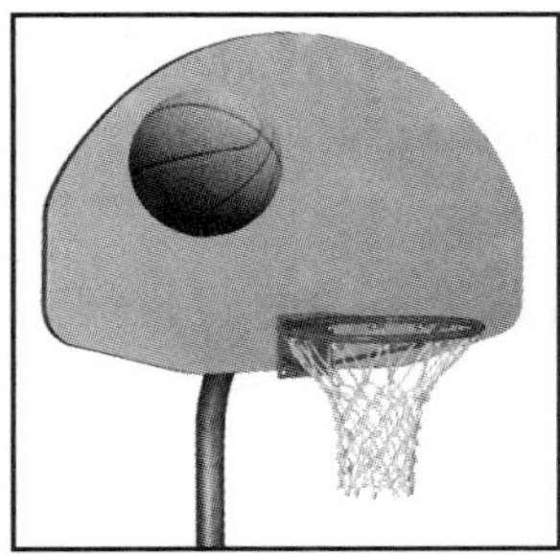

Act like you are playing basketball.

Act like you are using a compass.

Act like you are doing research at the library.

______________________ ______________ ______________________
Name   Date   Helper

Inferencing – Crossword

Instructions: Read each situation and question. Find the answer in the Word Bank and write it in the puzzle.

Word Bank

school	morning	doctor	exercising	judge
emailing	mall	microscope	astronaut	janitor

Across

4. The scientist looked through the eyepiece and viewed the bacteria on the slide. *What was the scientist looking through?*

6. Sam logged in and typed a message to his friend. *What was he doing?*

8. Sara grabbed her black bag with her stethoscope and thermometer. *What was Sara's job?*

9. We climbed in the shuttle and waited for the countdown. *What was your job?*

10. The sun was just beginning to rise in the sky. *What time of day was it?*

Down

1. You took your new notebooks and backpack with you on your first day. *Where were you going?*

2. Julie went up the escalator, past the food court, to the department store. *Where was she?*

3. The woman in the black robe called for order in the court. *What was her job?*

5. Mom did aerobics for 10 minutes, stretched, and lifted weights. *What was she doing?*

7. Danny emptied trash cans from all classrooms, swept the halls, and mopped the lunchroom. *What does Danny do?*

Name　　　　　Date　　　　　Helper

Inferencing – Word Search

Instructions: Read the questions, and then circle the answers in the puzzle. For help, use the Word Bank.

Word Bank

bank	sunrise	exercising	judge	school
binoculars	emailing	fall	compass	sick

```
I  G  L  D  S  V  F  S  E  E  A  O  D
K  O  K  O  I  I  U  V  G  F  A  L  L
L  M  B  J  O  N  C  J  D  J  Q  K  Z
N  J  T  I  R  H  J  K  U  E  Y  P  P
Q  N  A  I  N  X  C  I  J  B  G  C  E
C  T  S  H  Y  O  C  S  L  L  V  K  M
U  E  E  X  E  R  C  I  S  I  N  G  A
R  S  K  W  M  M  Z  U  K  Z  S  C  I
H  V  G  Q  O  R  Y  N  L  Z  H  C  L
Z  G  R  S  H  B  A  C  G  A  N  H  I
F  Y  S  B  X  B  B  Y  X  W  R  S  N
O  J  A  C  B  J  R  M  D  M  J  S  G
S  S  A  P  M  O  C  E  W  C  N  D  G
```

1. What time of the year was it?

2. What is her job?

3. What is he doing?

4. What is she doing?

5. What time of day is it?

6. Where was she?

7. What is wrong with Tommy?

8. What is she looking through?

9. Where were you going?

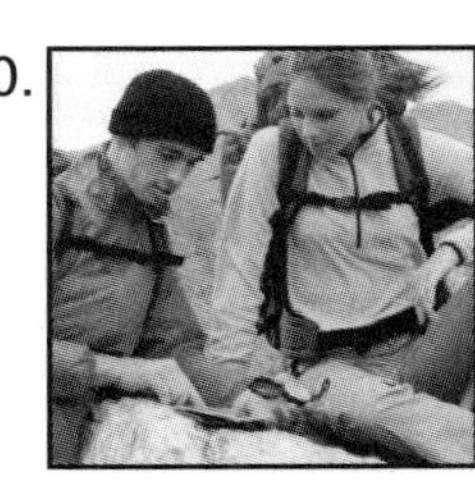

10. What did we use?

___________________   ___________________   ___________________
        Name   Date   Helper

Inferencing – Draw a Picture

Instructions: Read each situation and question. Then draw a picture in each box that answers the question.

1.

Tommy took his medicine and crawled into bed.
What is wrong with Tommy?

2.

The circus clown tossed the brightly colored
balls into the air without dropping any.
What was the clown doing?

3.

The teller counted the money and put it in the
vault. *Where was she?*

4.

The colorful leaves covered the ground.
What time of year was it?

5.

Mom was boiling water on the stove and
was distracted by the baby crying.
Why was this a problem?

6.

We love the dinosaur and the African animal
exhibits. *Where are we?*

Name   Date   Helper

Inferencing – Five Word Association

Instructions: Write five words that are associated with each photo.

A. 

1. _______________________
2. _______________________
3. _______________________
4. _______________________
5. _______________________

B. 

1. _______________________
2. _______________________
3. _______________________
4. _______________________
5. _______________________

C. 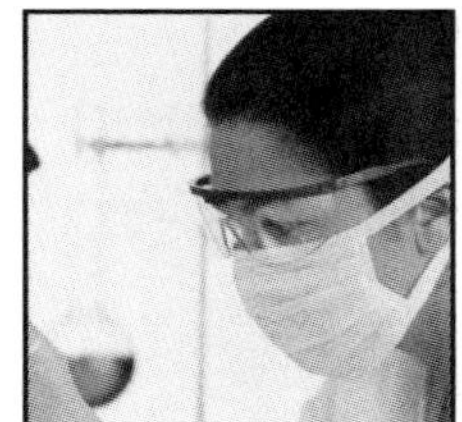

1. _______________________
2. _______________________
3. _______________________
4. _______________________
5. _______________________

D. 

1. _______________________
2. _______________________
3. _______________________
4. _______________________
5. _______________________

E. 

1. _______________________
2. _______________________
3. _______________________
4. _______________________
5. _______________________

F. 

1. _______________________
2. _______________________
3. _______________________
4. _______________________
5. _______________________

G. 

1. _______________________
2. _______________________
3. _______________________
4. _______________________
5. _______________________

H. 

1. _______________________
2. _______________________
3. _______________________
4. _______________________
5. _______________________

I. 

1. _______________________
2. _______________________
3. _______________________
4. _______________________
5. _______________________

_________________________ _________________________ _________________________
Name   Date   Helper

Inferencing – Fill It In

Instructions: Look at the photos. Then fill in the blanks with words from the Word Bank to complete the sentences. Tell what is going on in each situation.

______________________________ **Word Bank** ______________________________

scientist	boiling	hole	read	shot	needle
sun	dribble			stove	ball
bed	lost	medicine	eyepiece	sky	prize

1.  Mom was

   ____

   water on the

   ____

   and was distracted by the baby crying.

2. 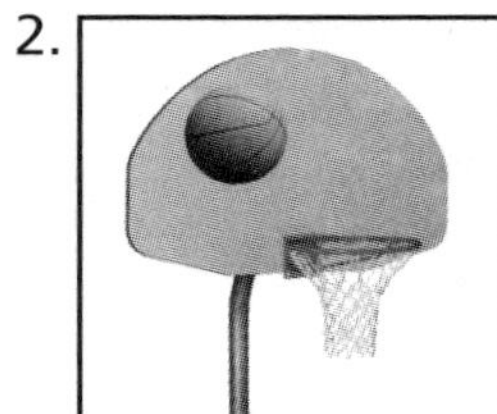 Johnny watched the player

   ____

   down the court and sink a three-point

   _________________________.

3.  Tommy took his

   ____

   and crawled into

   _________________________.

4.  Caleb drove the

   ____

   so far that it landed on the green next to the

   _________________________.

5. The _________________________

   looked through the

   ____

   and viewed the bacteria on the slide.

6.  The _________________________

   was just beginning to rise in the

   _________________________.

7. Joey _________________________

   150 books and won first

   ____

   in the fourth grade reading contest.

8. When we were

   _________________________,

   we looked at the

   ____

   on this to find our way.

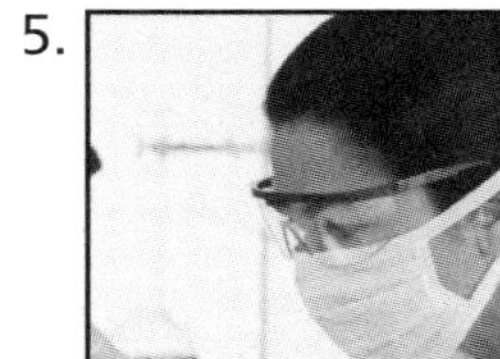

______________________   ______________________   ______________________
          Name   Date   Helper

Inferencing – Answering Why Questions

Instructions: Look at each photo and read the situation. Then answer the *Why* question that goes with each one.

1. The baby was playing with a bag of small marbles.
   Why was this a problem?

   ____

   ____

   ____

2. Joey read 150 books and won first prize in the fourth grade reading contest.
   Why did Joey win?

   ____

   ____

   ____

3. You left the windows open at your house, and it started raining.
   Why was this a problem?

   ____

   ____

   ____

4. Mom was boiling water on the stove and was distracted by the baby crying.
   Why was this a problem?

   ____

   ____

   ____

5. You cannot find your science textbook, and you have a test tomorrow.
   Why is this a problem?

   ____

   ____

   ____

_______________________ _______________________ _______________________
Name   Date   Helper

Inferencing – Ask a Question

Instructions: Look at each photo and read the answer. Then write a question you could ask to get that answer.

1. Question: ____

   ____ ?

   Answer: Mary did cartwheels, and Susan performed on the balance beam.

2. Question: ____

   ____ ?

   Answer: Julie went up the escalator, past the food court, to the department store.

3. Question: ____

   ____ ?

   Answer: We love the dinosaur and the African animal exhibits.

4. Question: ____

   ____ ?

   Answer: We dressed in red, white, and blue clothes and watched the fireworks display.

5. Question: ____

   ____ ?

   Answer: We checked in and got our room keys.

Name   Date   Helper

Inferencing – Decode the Word

Instructions: Fill in each blank with the correct word. For help, use the Word Bank. Then transfer each letter that has a number under it to reveal the *Secret Word*.

Word Bank

basketball

marbles

backpack

umbrella

leaves

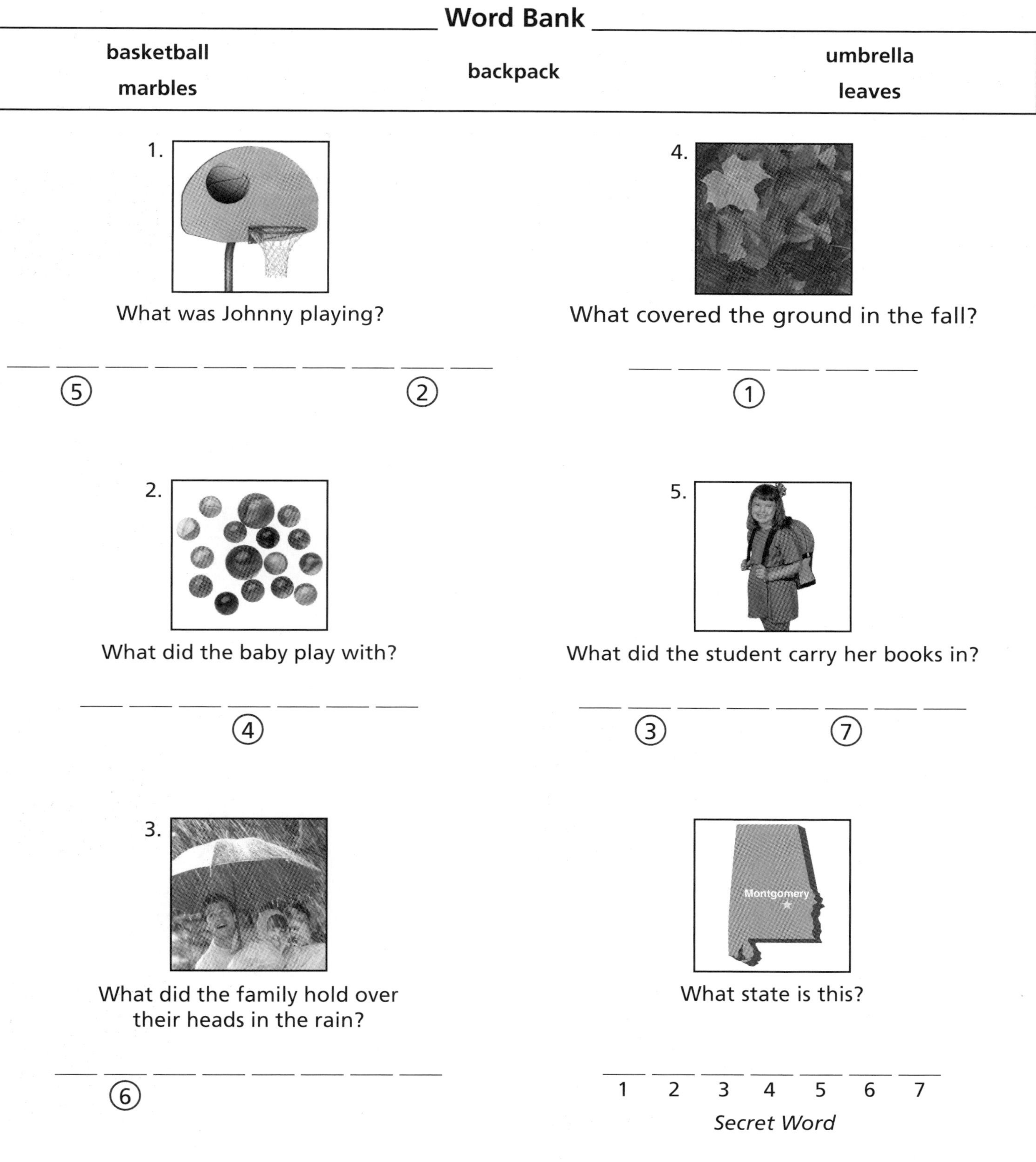

1. What was Johnny playing?

— — — — — — — — — —
⑤   ②

2. What did the baby play with?

— — — — — — —
        ④

3. What did the family hold over their heads in the rain?

— — — — — — — —
    ⑥

4. What covered the ground in the fall?

— — — — — —
        ①

5. What did the student carry her books in?

— — — — — — — —
    ③   ⑦

— — — — — — —
1   2   3   4   5   6   7

Secret Word

___________________   ___________________   ___________________
Name   Date   Helper

Inferencing – Right or Wrong Inference?

Instructions: Read each situation. If the inference is right, color the *happy* face. If the inference is wrong, color the *sad* face. For every sad face, give a correct inference.

1. Danny emptied trash cans from all classrooms, swept the halls, and mopped the lunchroom.
   Inference: Danny keeps the school clean.

2. We checked in and got our room keys.
   Inference: We were at the hotel.

3. The sun was just beginning to rise in the sky.
   Inference: It was sunset.

4. The scientist looked through the eyepiece and viewed the bacteria on the slide.
   Inference: She was looking through a camera.

5. Sara grabbed her black bag with her stethoscope and thermometer.
   Inference: Sara is a doctor.

6. When we were lost, we looked at the needle on this to find our way.
   Inference: We looked at a cell phone.

7. Mom did aerobics for 10 minutes, stretched, and lifted weights.
   Inference: Mom was working out.

8. Charlie grabbed his tool belt and drill and went to work.
   Inference: Charlie is a teacher.

Name	Date	Helper

Inferencing – Story Writer

Instructions: Look at the photos and write a short story about each one. Think about *who*, *what*, and *where* for each story.

1. 

____

____

____

____

2. 

____

____

____

____

3.

____

____

____

____

Name	Date	Helper

Inferencing – What Is It?

Instructions: Look at each photo and read the situation that goes with it. Then write a definition for the word in *italics*.

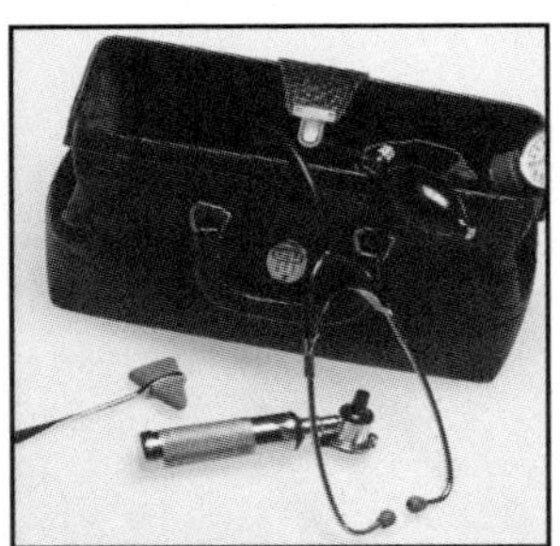

1. Sara grabbed her black bag with her stethoscope and *thermometer*.

   Definition: ____

   ____

   ____

2. Charlie grabbed his *tool belt* and drill and went to work.

   Definition: ____

   ____

   ____

3. We climbed in the *shuttle* and waited for the countdown.

   Definition: ____

   ____

   ____

4. Mom was boiling water on the stove and was *distracted* by the baby crying.

   Definition: ____

   ____

   ____

5. The teller counted the money and put it in the *vault*.

   Definition: ____

   ____

   ____

Name	Date	Helper

Inferencing – What Else?

Instructions: Look at each photo and read the situation that goes with it. Then write what else could be happening in the situation.

1. Sam is emailing. *What else could Sam be doing?*

____

____

____

2. She is going to school. *Where else could she be going?*

____

____

____

3. We used a compass to find our way. *What else could we use?*

____

____

____

4. John was doing research at the library. *What else could he be doing at the library?*

____

____

____

5. It is morning. *What other time of day could it be?*

____

____

____

Name _______________ Date _______________ Helper _______________

Inferencing – Questions

Instructions: Read each statement below. Then answer the question that goes with it.

1. It was the Fourth of July. *Why do people wear red, white, and blue on this day?*

____

____

____

2. Mom was exercising. *What else should you do to stay healthy?*

____

____

____

3. Charlie is a construction worker. *Why does Charlie need a tool belt?*

____

____

____

4. Nicole was looking through binoculars. *How are telescopes and binoculars alike?*

____

____

____

5. The woman is a judge. *What does it mean to listen to "both sides of a story"?*

____

____

____

_________________________   ___________   _________________________
Name   Date   Helper

Determining Perspective – Match It Up

Instructions: Read each thought below. Under each photo write the number of the thought that matches it. Then circle the words in the sentences that gave you clues.

A.   B.   C.   D.

E.   F.   G.   H.

1. Fido is such a great pet.

2. Oh no, I'm late!

3. I wish they would stop arguing.

4. Oh no, it's too short!

5. I can't believe the Yankees just lost the game.

6. Oh no, I deleted my whole report!

7. I'm so happy we won the championship!

8. I can't wait until this dinner party is over.

___________________   ___________________   ___________________
Name   Date   Helper

Determining Perspective – Memory Game

Instructions: Cut out the cards. Shuffle and place all cards facedown. Player One chooses two cards to try to match the photo card with the corresponding thought card. Player Two follows in turn. The player with the most matches wins.

I couldn't swim fast enough.	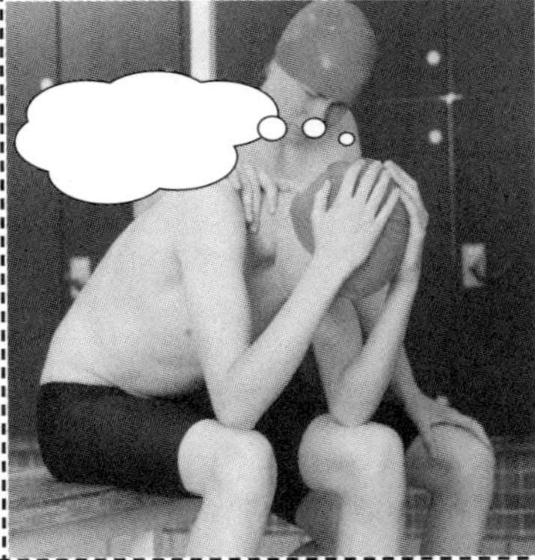	Peas are disgusting!	
I don't understand social studies.		Are these worms?	
I'm so lonely.		Hey, where's my drink?	
You're such a good dog.		This math is too tough for me.	

______________________   ______________________   ______________________
Name   Date   Helper

Determining Perspective – Where Was the Photo Taken?

Instructions: Read each statement and find the photo on the map that matches it. Then write the name of the city where the photo was taken.

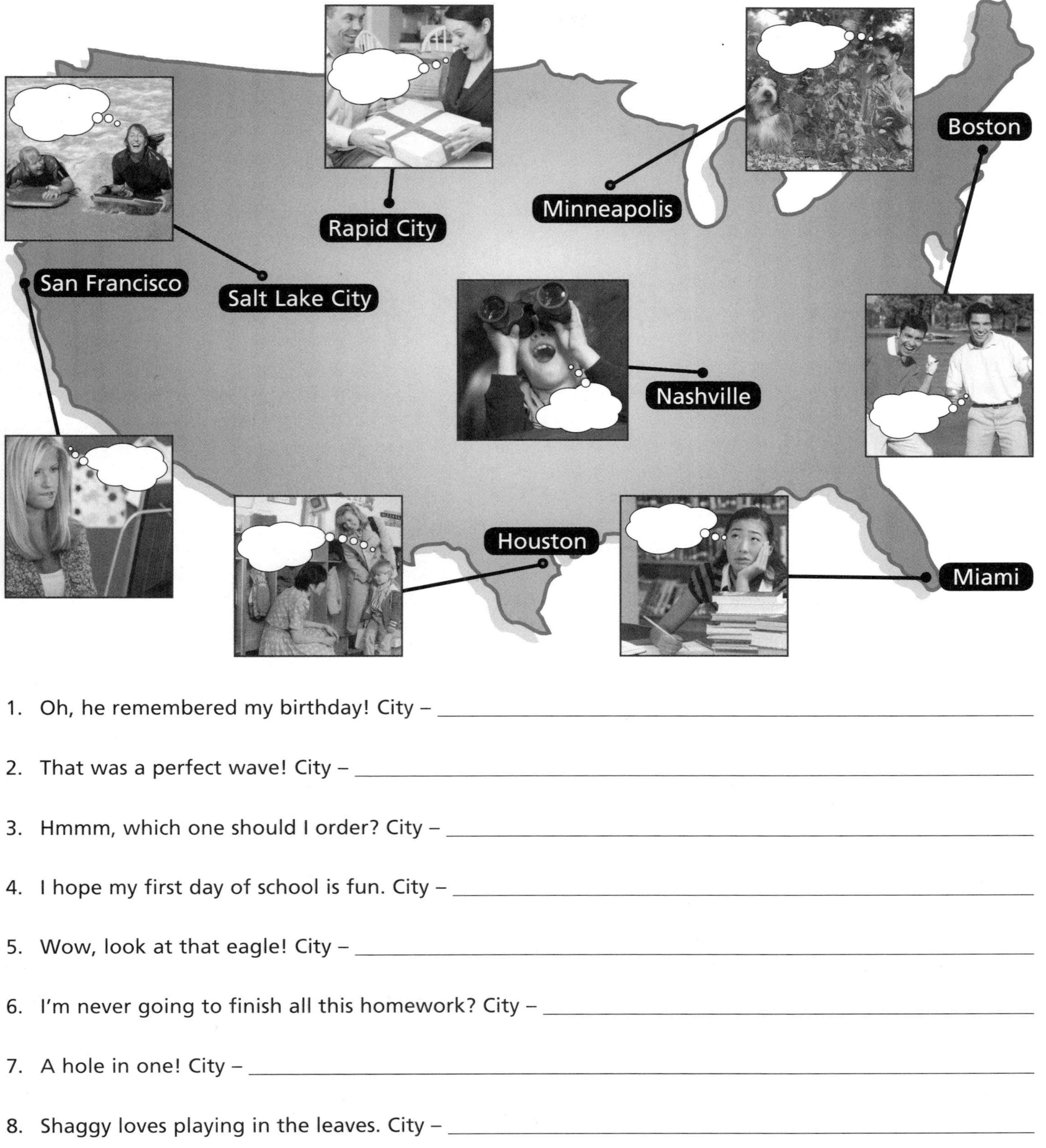

1. Oh, he remembered my birthday! City – ____

2. That was a perfect wave! City – ____

3. Hmmm, which one should I order? City – ____

4. I hope my first day of school is fun. City – ____

5. Wow, look at that eagle! City – ____

6. I'm never going to finish all this homework? City – ____

7. A hole in one! City – ____

8. Shaggy loves playing in the leaves. City – ____

_______________________________   _______________________   _______________________________
             Name   Date   Helper

Determining Perspective – The Best Perspective

Instructions: Look at each photo, and circle the best perspective that goes in the thought bubble.

1. What is he thinking?

   A. What's for dinner?

   B. I can't eat this!

   C. I love sushi!

2. What is he thinking?

   A. I love recess!

   B. Hmm, what was my best vacation?

   C. Math is hard.

3. What is she thinking?

   A. I don't understand how to use this.

   B. Art is my favorite class.

   C. I wonder what's for lunch today.

4. What is he thinking?

   A. I love my red Mustang.

   B. Road trips are so much fun!

   C. I hope the tow truck comes soon.

5. What is he thinking?

   A. I missed her so much!

   B. These fatigues are comfortable.

   C. I'm leaving on the next plane.

Name   Date   Helper

Determining Perspective – What's on Their Minds?

Instructions: To assemble the cube, cut on the dotted lines. Fold on the solid line, and glue/tape as indicated. To play, roll the cube. Look at the photo on the top side of the cube. Tell what the person is thinking.

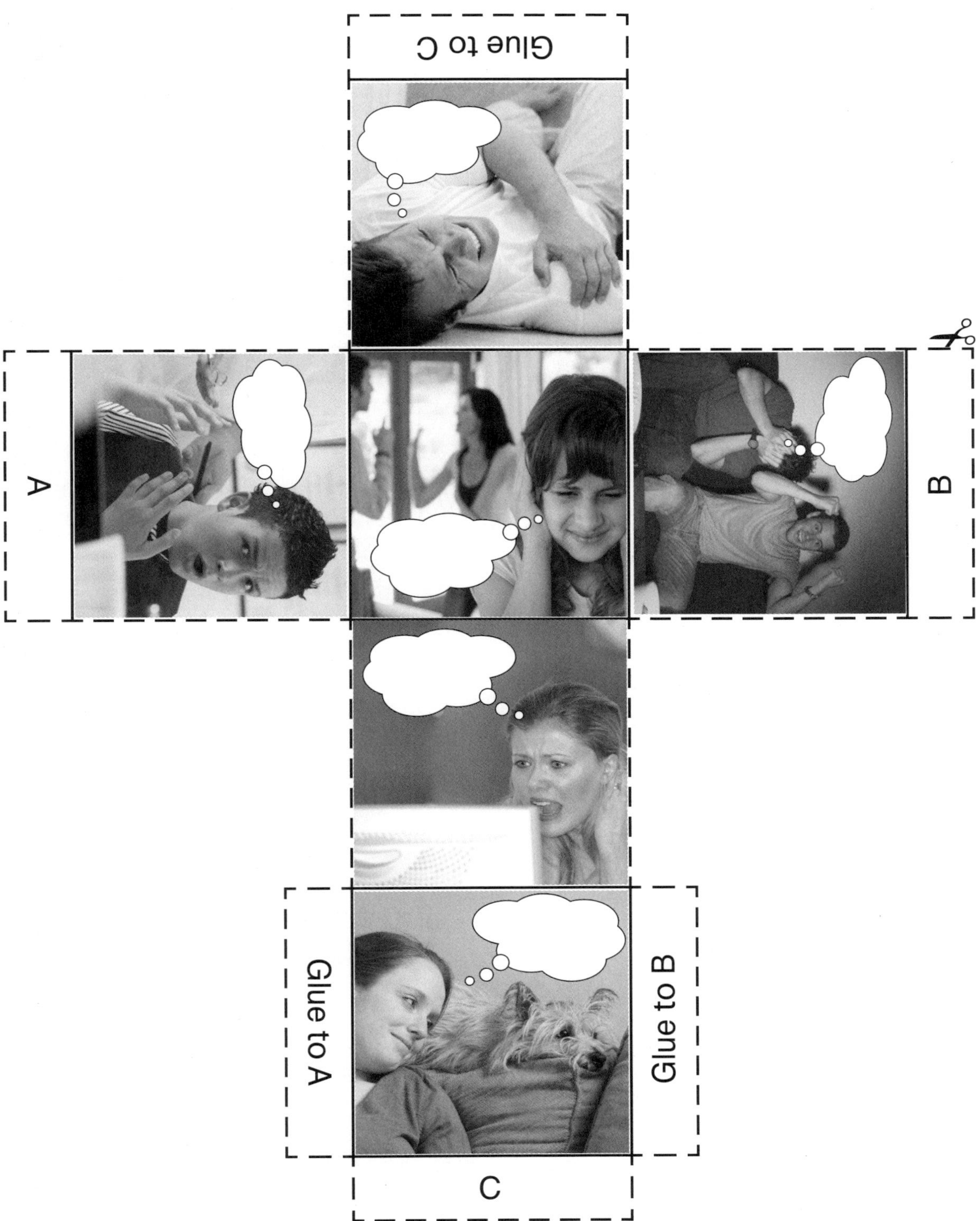

Name   Date   Helper

Determining Perspective – How Do They Feel?

Instructions: Cut out the photos at the bottom of the page. Then glue/tape each photo next to the emotion that goes with it.

1. lonely

4. upset 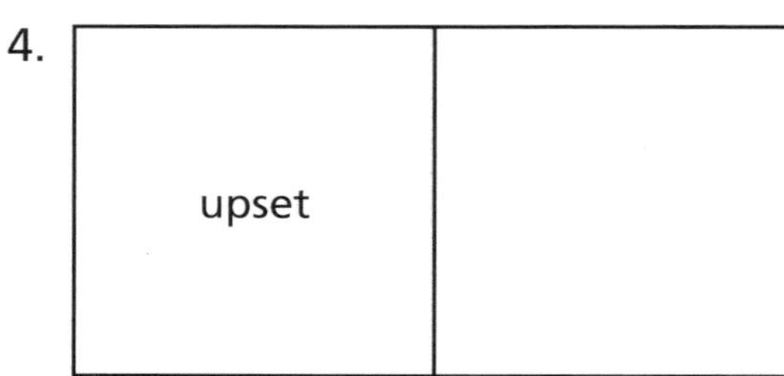

2. annoyed

5. surprised 

3. bored

6. proud

___________________   ___________________   ___________________
Name   Date   Helper

     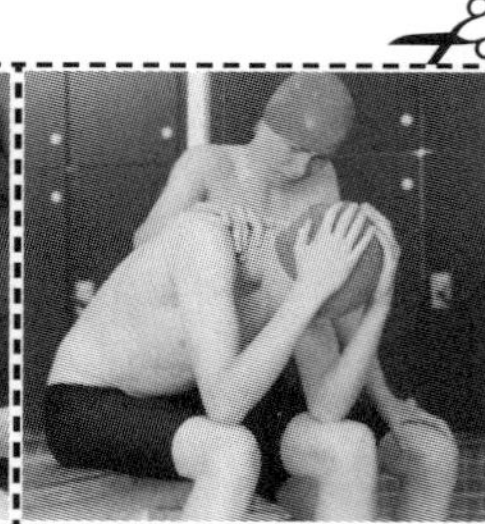

#BK-374 *The Question Challenge™ Card Game Fun Sheets* • ©2012 Super Duper® Publications • www.superduperinc.com • 1-800-277-8737

Determining Perspective – Tic-Tac-Toe

Instructions: Cut out the tic-tac-toe markers below. Take turns placing your markers in the boxes, and tell what you think each person is thinking. The first player to get three in a row (tic-tac-toe) wins.

Name   Date   Helper

Determining Perspective – Act It Out

Instructions: Cut out the cards. Shuffle and place all cards facedown. Player One chooses a card and acts it out. Other players try to guess what Player One is thinking. Play continues in turn.

Name

Date

Helper

Determining Perspective – Crossword

Instructions: Look at each photo and find the word in the Word Bank that describes what the person is feeling. Write the answers in the puzzle.

─── **Word Bank** ───

excited	impatient	discouraged	relaxed	disgusted
playful	happy	puzzled	disappointed	nervous

Across

1.    5.    8.    9.    10.

Down

2.

3.

4.

6.

7.

Determining Perspective – Unscramble

Instructions: Unscramble each sentence to tell what the person is thinking.

1.

old   breaks   down   This   always   car

____ .

2.

hope   drink   I   she   my   next   brings

____ .

3.

going   I'm   be   to   again   late

____ .

4.

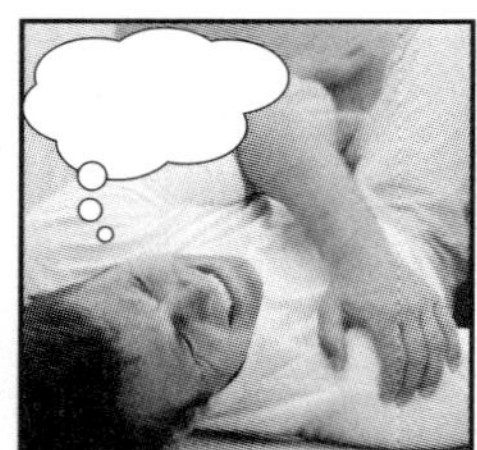

my   arm   broken   think   I   is

____ .

5.

off   Those   paid   lessons   golf

____ .

____________________________ ____________ ____________________________
       Name   Date   Helper

Determining Perspective – Draw a Picture

Instructions: Read each situation below. Then draw a picture in the box that illustrates what each person is thinking.

1.

Grandpa bought Susie a present.
What is she thinking?

4.

Max saw a huge bird in the sky.
What is he thinking?

2.

Mike tripped and hurt his shoulder.
What is he thinking?

5.

Debbie had so much reading to do.
What is she thinking?

3.

Kim just won a trophy.
What is she thinking?

6.

Charlie was resting with his dog.
What is he thinking?

Name   Date   Helper

Determining Perspective – Five Word Association

Instructions: Write five words that are associated with each photo.

A. 

1. _______________________
2. _______________________
3. _______________________
4. _______________________
5. _______________________

B. 

1. _______________________
2. _______________________
3. _______________________
4. _______________________
5. _______________________

C. 

1. _______________________
2. _______________________
3. _______________________
4. _______________________
5. _______________________

D. 

1. _______________________
2. _______________________
3. _______________________
4. _______________________
5. _______________________

E. 

1. _______________________
2. _______________________
3. _______________________
4. _______________________
5. _______________________

F. 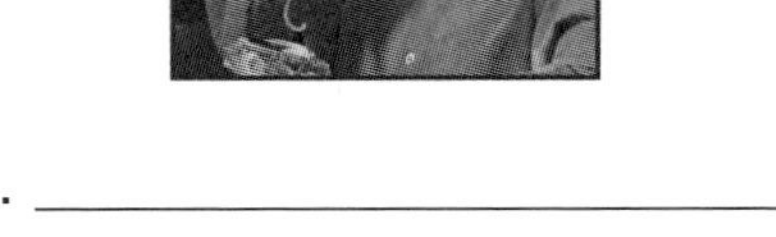

1. _______________________
2. _______________________
3. _______________________
4. _______________________
5. _______________________

G. 

1. _______________________
2. _______________________
3. _______________________
4. _______________________
5. _______________________

H. 

1. _______________________
2. _______________________
3. _______________________
4. _______________________
5. _______________________

I. 

1. _______________________
2. _______________________
3. _______________________
4. _______________________
5. _______________________

_______________________   _______________________   _______________________
Name   Date   Helper

Determining Perspective – Fill It In

Instructions: Look at the photos. Then fill in the blanks with words from the Word Bank to complete the thoughts.

Word Bank

virus	deserted			beautiful	autumn
sideburns	computer	sushi	short	bouquet	disgusting
high	playing	multiplication	friends	waves	math

1. Oh no, I think I have a

   ____

   on my

   _________________________ !

5. This

   ____

   looks

   _________________________ .

2. He cut my

   ____

   so

   _________________________ !

6. My

   ____

   have all

   _________________________ me.

3. The

   ____

   are very

   _________________________ today!

7. _________________________

   is a difficult

   _________________________ concept.

4. I love

   ____

   in the

   ____

   leaves with Shaggy.

8. My

   ____

   wife deserves this lovely

   _________________________ .

_________________________   _________________________   _________________________

Name   Date   Helper

Determining Perspective – Answering Why Questions

Instructions: Look at the photos, and answer the *Why* questions.

1. Why is she covering her ears?

____

____

____

2. Why is he holding his shoulder?

____

____

3. Why is he sitting on his car?

____

____

4. Why is he looking down and holding his head?

____

____

5. Why is she sticking out her tongue?

____

____

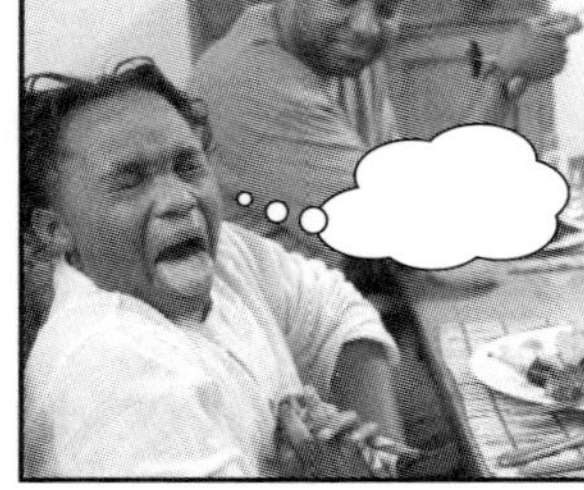

Name	Date	Helper

#BK-374 *The Question Challenge™ Card Game Fun Sheets* • ©2012 Super Duper® Publications • www.superduperinc.com • 1-800-277-8737

Determining Perspective – Ask a Question

Instructions: Look at each photo and read the answer. Then write a question you could ask to get that answer.

1. Question: _________________________________

   ____ ?

   Answer: My team lost 0–10.

2. Question: _________________________________

   ____ ?

   Answer: I was supposed to get up an hour ago.

3. Question: _________________________________

   ____ ?

   Answer: My name is Thomas Smith.

4. Question: _________________________________

   ____ ?

   Answer: The eagle is in the tree.

5. Question: _________________________________

   ____ ?

   Answer: I'm writing a story about my summer vacation.

Name	Date	Helper

Determining Perspective – Decode the Word

Instructions: Fill in each blank with the correct word. For help, use the Word Bank. Then transfer each letter that has a number under it to reveal the *Secret Word*. Then look at the pictures and tell how you think each person feels.

Word Bank

haircut
abacus
fight
binoculars
multiplication

1.

I hate it when they

___ ___ ___ ___ ___.
    ②

2.

This ___ ___ ___ ___ ___ ___
    ⑦
is too short!

3.

___ ___ ___ ___ ___ ___ ___ ___
①   ⑧
is so difficult.

4.

I don't know how to use this

___ ___ ___ ___ ___ ___.
       ③

5.

___ ___ ___ ___ ___ ___ ___ ___ ___ ___
    ⑤   ⑥   ④
are amazing!

What state is this?

___ ___ ___ ___ ___ ___ ___ ___
1 2 3 4 5 6 7 8

Secret Word

___________________ ___________ ___________
Name   Date   Helper

Determining Perspective – Right or Wrong Perspective?

Instructions: Read each statement. If the perspective is correct, color the *happy* face. If the perspective is incorrect, color the *sad* face. For every sad face, give a correct perspective.

 1. You are such an annoying dog. 

 2. I've never seen food like this before. 

 3. I hope she didn't forget my drink! 

 4. Math is so easy! 

 5. I just hate homework. 

 6. I'm so afraid of sharks! 

 7. I'll have to rake all these leaves again. 

 8. I wonder what he got me! 

______________________ ____________ ______________________
Name   Date   Helper

Determining Perspective – Story Writer

Instructions: Look at the photos and write a short story about each one. Write about what each person is thinking and feeling. Consider *who, what,* and *where* for each story.

1.

2.

3.

Name   Date   Helper

Determining Perspective – What Is It?

Instructions: Look at each photo and read the thought that goes with it. Then write a definition for the word in *italics*.

1. My favorite *soldier* is home!

   Definition: _______________________________________

   ____

   ____

2. This dinner party is so *boring*.

   Definition: _______________________________________

   ____

   ____

3. Something strange is happening to my *computer*.

   Definition: _______________________________________

   ____

   ____

4. I can't wait to show my mom this *trophy*.

   Definition: _______________________________________

   ____

   ____

5. I love playing in the *autumn* leaves with Shaggy.

   Definition: _______________________________________

   ____

   ____

_______________________ _______________ _______________________
Name   Date   Helper

Determining Perspective – What Else Could They Be Thinking?

Instructions: Look at each photo and read the thought that goes with it. Then write what else the person could be thinking in that situation.

1. I think I will write in my journal about my trip to the Grand Canyon.
   What else could he be thinking?

   ____

   ____

   ____

2. I wish I could remember my multiplication tables!
   What else could she be thinking?

   ____

   ____

   ____

3. Should I buy this dress online or not?
   What else could she be thinking?

   ____

   ____

   ____

4. You're such a good dog!
   What else could he be thinking?

   ____

   ____

   ____

5. I have no idea what to write about.
   What else could she be thinking?

   ____

   ____

   ____

_______________________   _______________________   _______________________
Name   Date   Helper

Stating Opinions – Match It Up

Instructions: Read each statement below. Under each photo write the number of the statement that matches it. Then give your opinion for each statement.

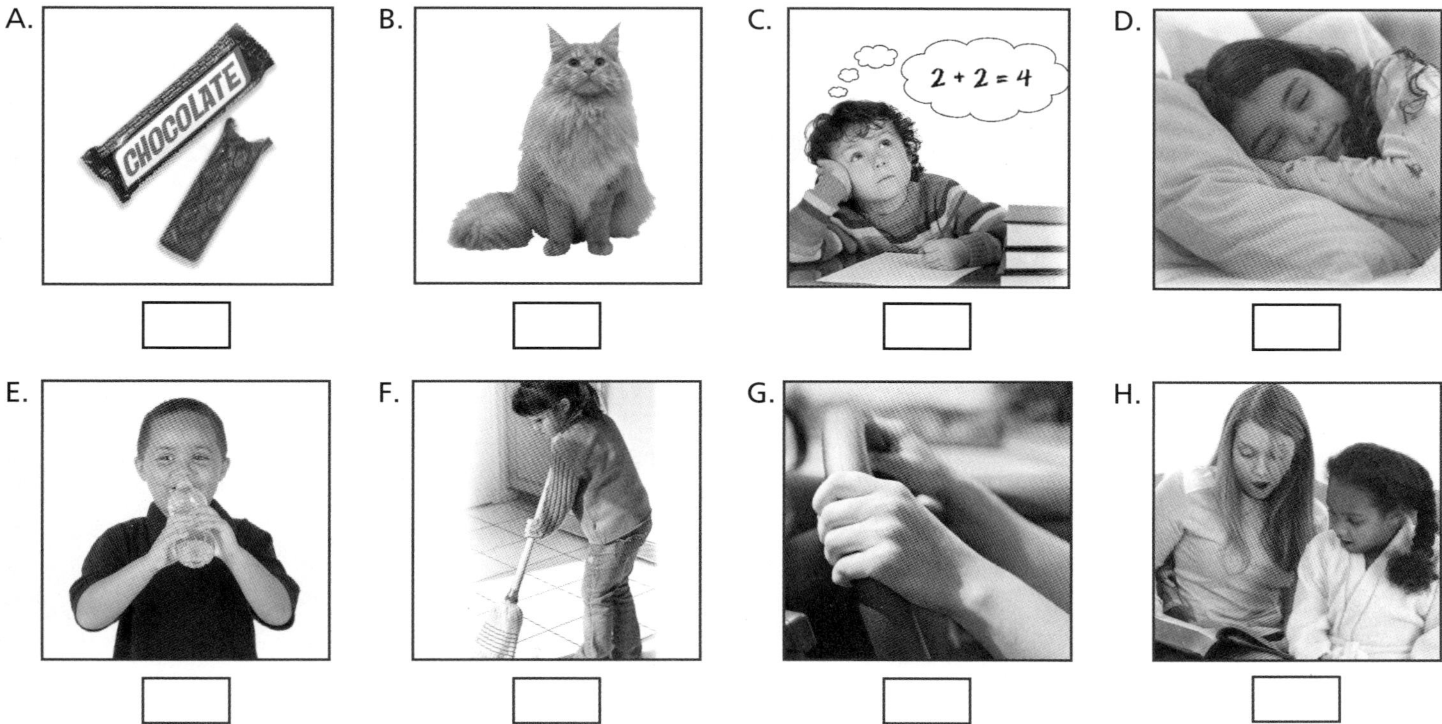

A. B. C. D.

E. F. G. H.

1. All children should do three hours of chores every Saturday.

2. Schools should not sell students sugary snacks.

3. People should be able to drive when they are fourteen years old.

4. Math is easier than social studies.

5. Students should not be allowed to bring water bottles to school.

6. Any child under 13 years old should have a babysitter.

7. Cats are better pets than dogs.

8. Everyone should go to bed at 8:00 p.m.

Name	Date	Helper

Stating Opinions – Memory Game

Instructions: Cut out the cards. Shuffle and place all cards facedown. Player One chooses two cards to try to match the photo card with the corresponding statement card. Player Two follows in turn. The player with the most matches wins. Give your opinion every time you make match.

Students should not be allowed to have cell phones.		Everyone should exercise two hours each day.	
Everyone on the team should get to play in the football game.		Students should go to school all year long.	
People should not date until they are 18 years old.		Thanksgiving is the best holiday.	
Video games do not teach you anything.	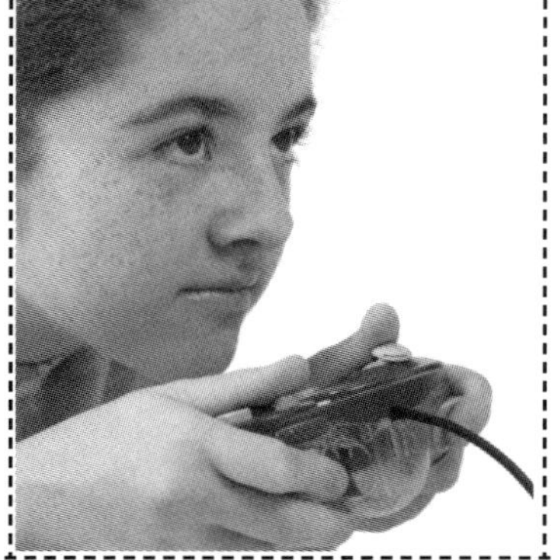	Only healthy treats should be given on Halloween — no candy.	

Name   Date   Helper

Stating Opinions – Where Was the Photo Taken?

Instructions: Read each statement and find the photo on the map that matches it. Then write the name of the city where the photo was taken. Give your opinion for each statement.

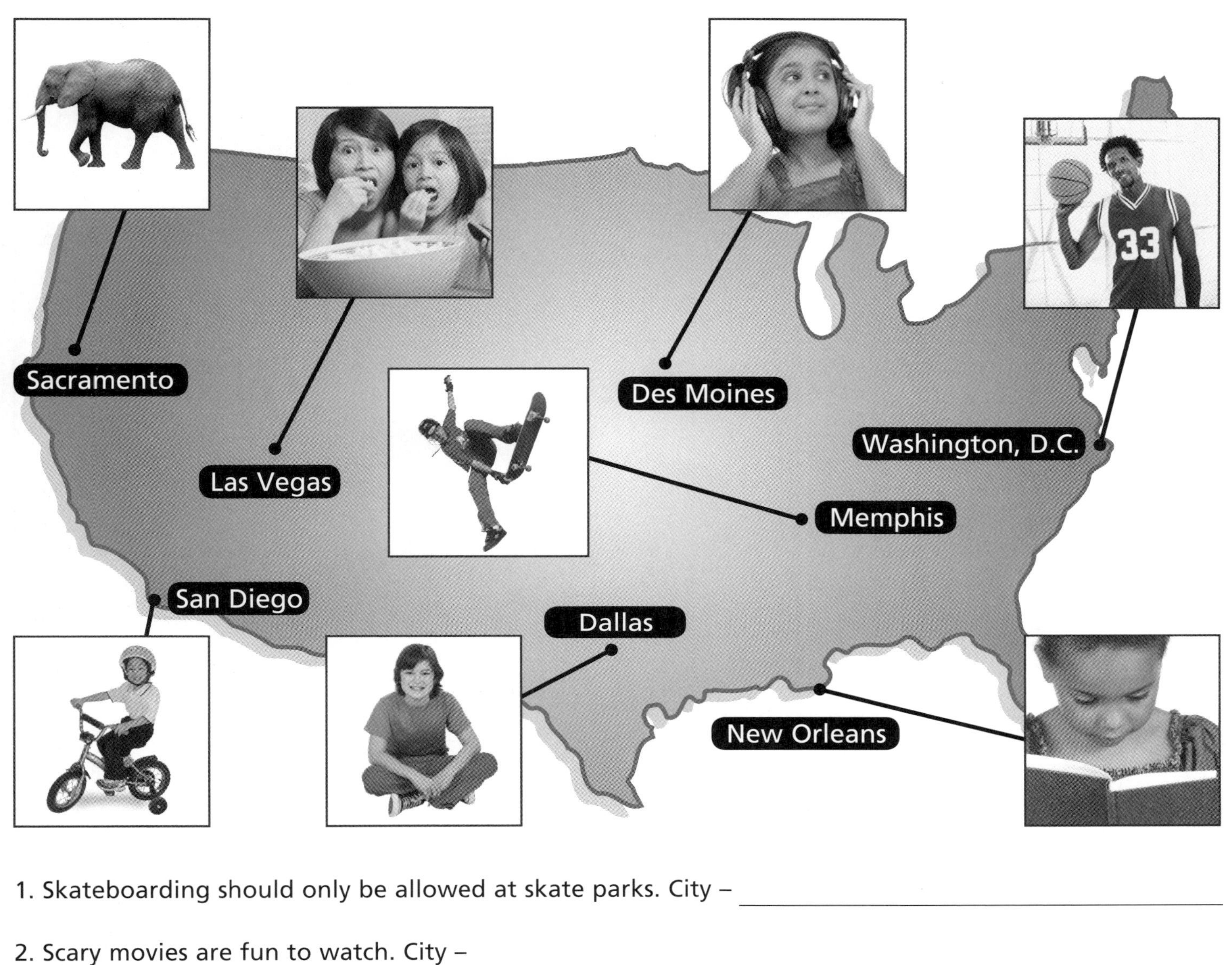

1. Skateboarding should only be allowed at skate parks. City – _______________________________

2. Scary movies are fun to watch. City – _______________________________

3. You should be able to choose whether you wear a bicycle helmet or not. City – _______________

4. Rap music is better than rock music. City – _______________________________

5. Elephants are the most interesting of all zoo animals. City – _______________________________

6. Green is the best color for T-shirts. City – _______________________________

7. Students should read two hours each night. City – _______________________________

8. Professional athletes make too much money. City – _______________________________

_______________________________ _______________ _______________

Name   Date   Helper

Stating Opinions – Find the Opinion Card

Instructions: Cut out the cards. Shuffle and place them facedown. Player One flips a card, reads the statement, and gives his/her opinion. Player Two follows in turn. First player to find the Opinion Card wins.

Students should only watch one television program on school nights.

Cereal is a better breakfast than eggs.

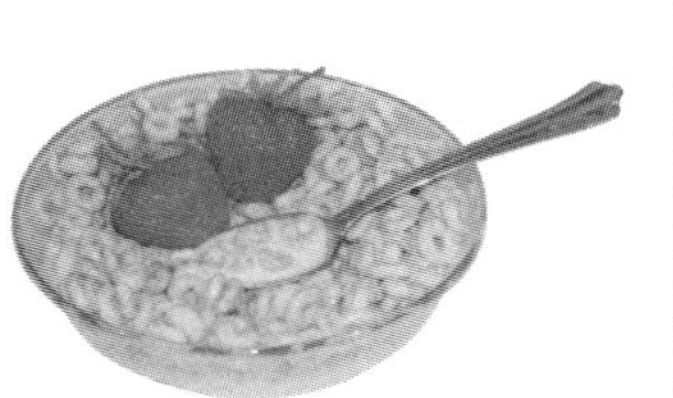

You should not get an allowance for helping out at home.

All students should take cell phones to school.

Camping is the best type of vacation.

Students should get report cards every week.

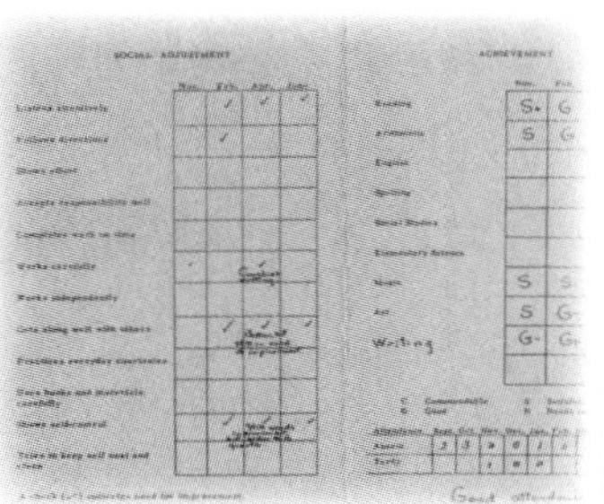

Students should go to school all year long.

Schools should not sell students sugary snacks.

People should be able to drive when they are fourteen years old.

Everyone on the team should get to play in the football game.

Cats are better pets than dogs.

Math is easier than social studies.

Green is the best color for T-shirts.

Everyone should go to bed at 8:00 p.m.

Students should not be allowed to bring water bottles to school.

______________________   ______________   ______________________
Name   Date   Helper

Stating Opinions – What Do You Think?

Instructions: To assemble the cube, cut on the dotted lines. Fold on the solid lines and glue/tape as indicated. To play, roll the cube. Read the statement on the top side of the cube. Give your opinion about the statement.

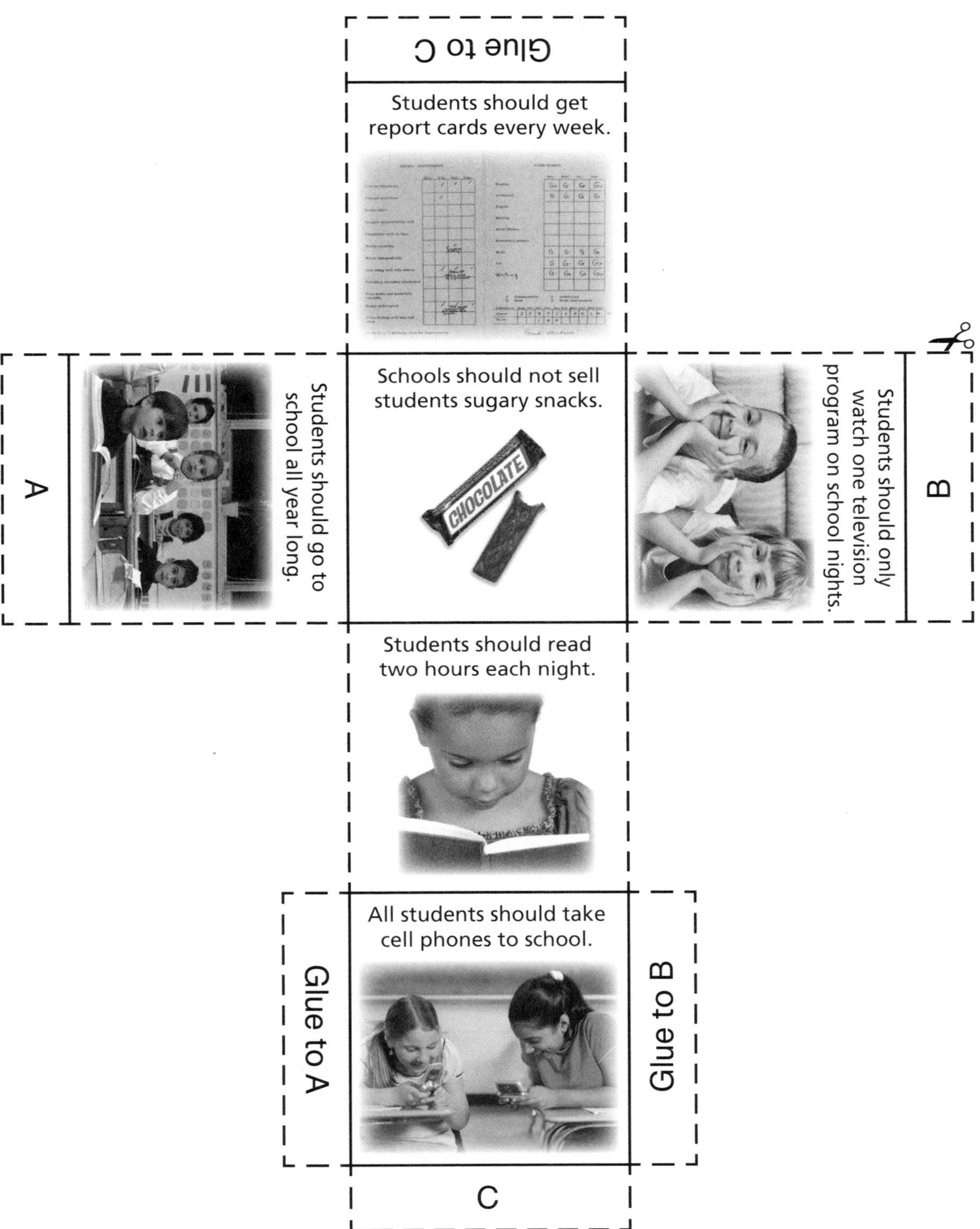

___________________________   ___________________   ___________________

Name   Date   Helper

Stating Opinions – Half-Match

Instructions: Cut out the photos/statements at the bottom of the page. Then tape/glue them under the matching photos/statements. Do you agree or disagree with the statements?

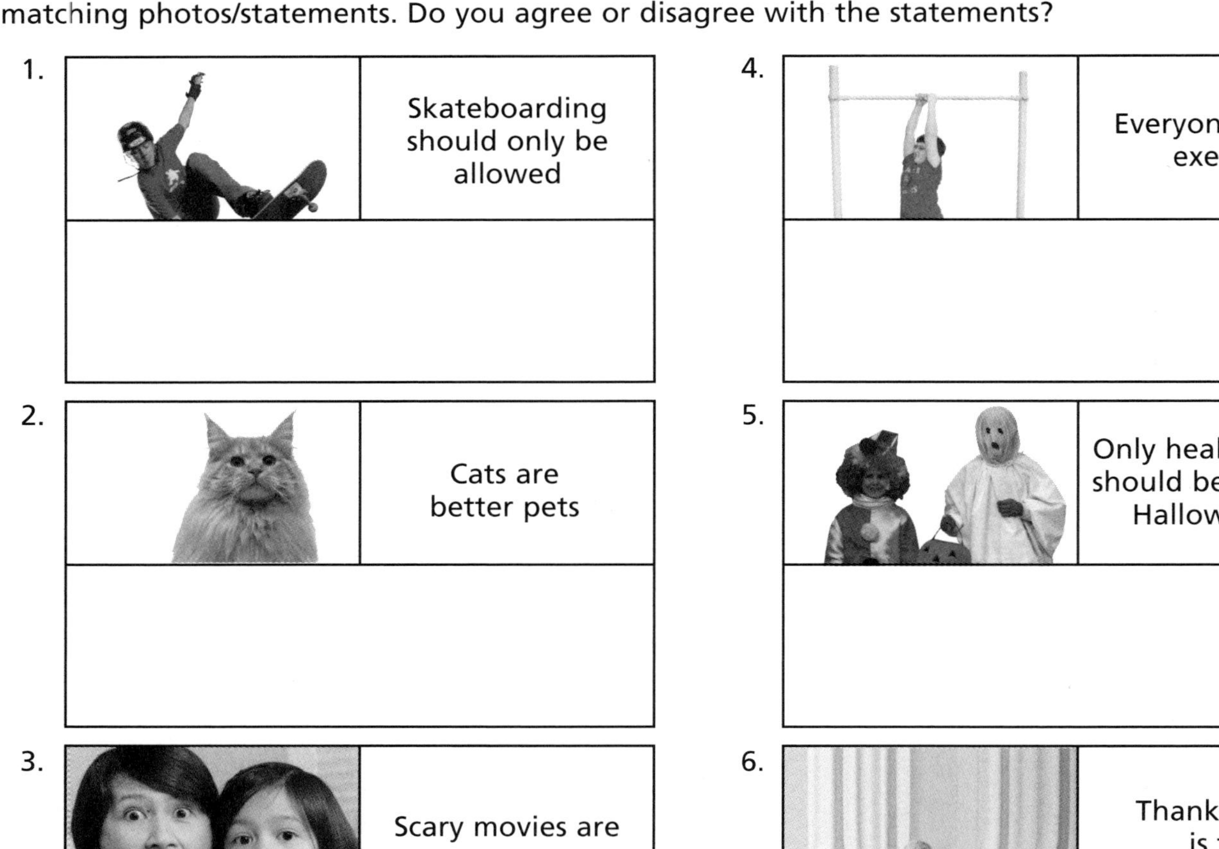

1. Skateboarding should only be allowed

4. Everyone should exercise

2. Cats are better pets

5. Only healthy treats should be given on Halloween —

3. Scary movies are

6. Thanksgiving is the

Name   Date   Helper ✂

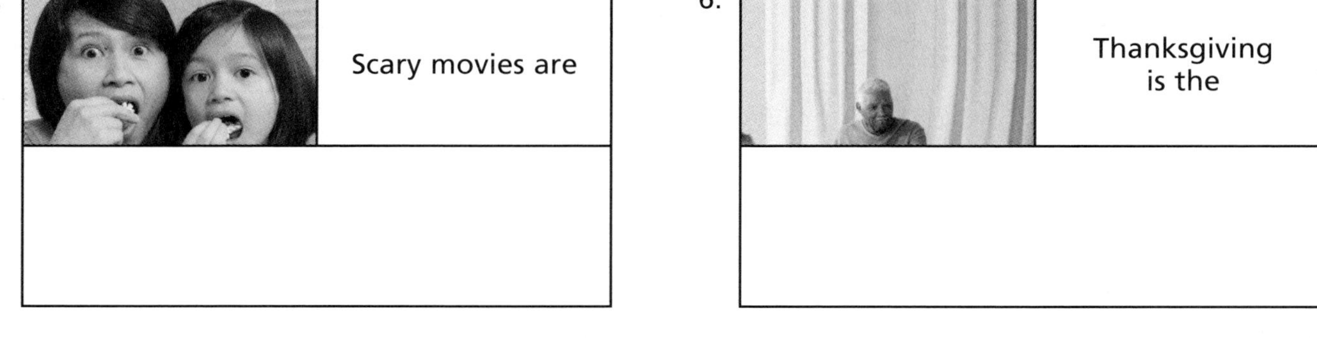

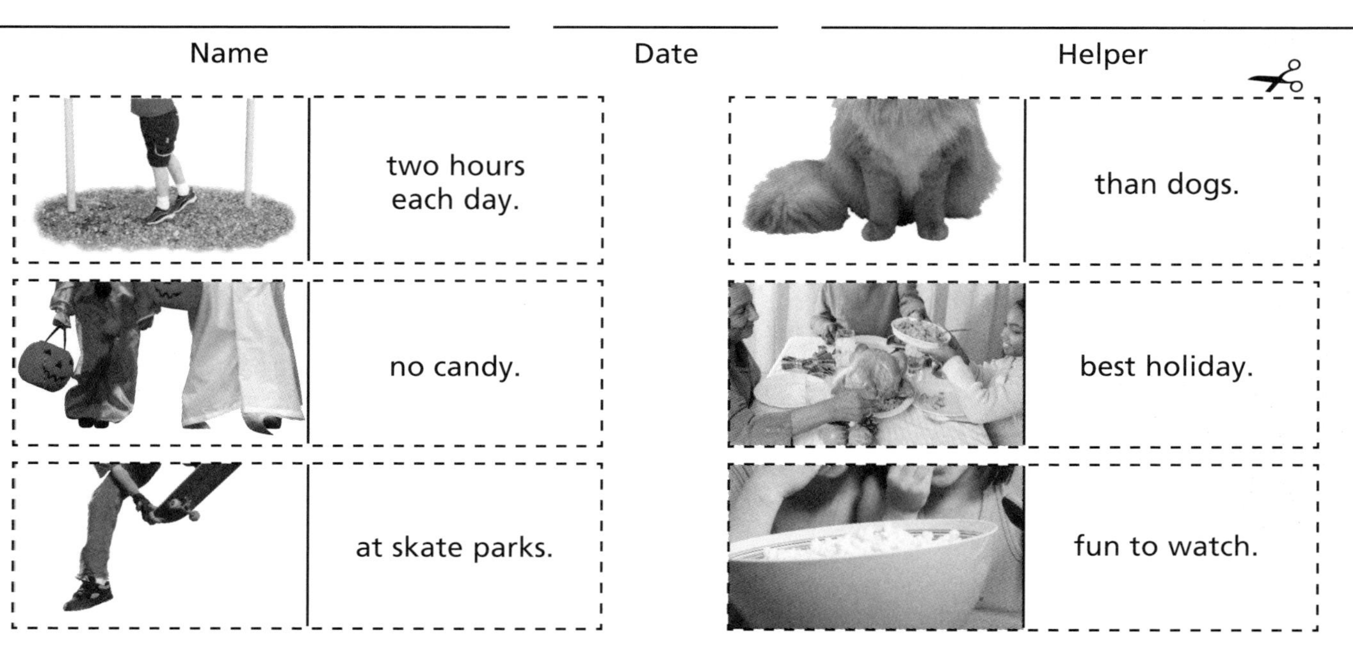

two hours each day.

than dogs.

no candy.

best holiday.

at skate parks.

fun to watch.

Stating Opinions – Game Board

Instructions: To play, cut out game pieces below and place them at "Start." Flip a coin to move. Heads – 1 space. Tails – 2 spaces. As you move around the board give your opinion for each statement you land on. The first player to reach "Finish" wins.

All children should do three hours of chores every Saturday. 	People should not date until they are 18 years old. 	Cereal is a better breakfast than eggs. 	Any child under 13 years old should have a babysitter. 	Students should not be allowed to have cell phones. 
START				Everyone should exercise two hours each day. 
Thanksgiving is the best holiday. 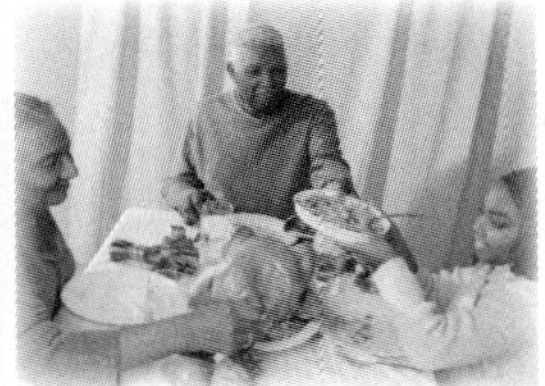	Rap music is better than rock music. 	You should be able to choose whether you wear a bicycle helmet or not. 	Camping is the best type of vacation. 	You should not get an allowance for helping out at home. 
Video games do not teach you anything. 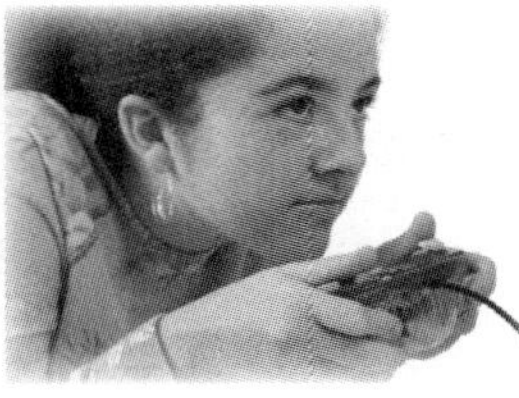				**FINISH**
Professional athletes make too much money.	Only healthy treats should be given on Halloween — no candy. 	Skateboarding should only be allowed at skate parks. 	Scary movies are fun to watch. 	Elephants are the most interesting of all zoo animals. 

Name   Date   Helper

Player 1

Player 2

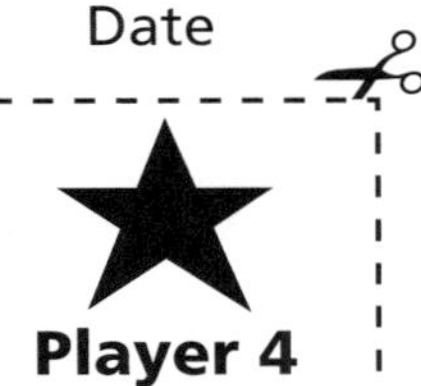

Player 3

Player 4

Stating Opinions – Tic-Tac-Toe

Instructions: Cut out the tic-tac-toe markers below. Take turns reading the statement in each box. Give your opinion as you place your marker in a box. The first player to get three in a row (tic-tac-toe) wins.

Elephants are the most interesting of all zoo animals. 	People should be able to drive when they are fourteen years old. 	Students should not be allowed to bring water bottles to school. 
Any child under 13 years old should have a babysitter. 	You should be able to choose whether you wear a bicycle helmet or not. 	Video games do not teach you anything. 
Students should get report cards every week. 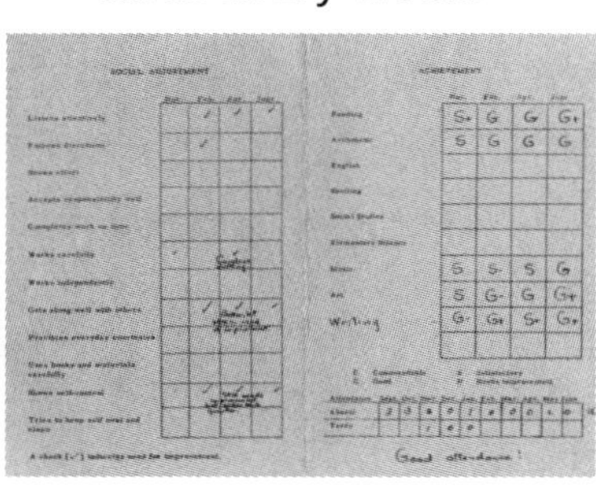	Everyone on the team should get to play in the football game.	Everyone should go to bed at 8:00 p.m.

Name   Date   Helper

X X X X X X

O O O O O O

Stating Opinions – Crossword

Instructions: Read each statement and find the word in the Word Bank that means the same as the word(s) below the blank. Write the answer in the puzzle. Give your opinion for each statement.

─── **Word Bank** ───

allowance	holiday	elephants	games	chores
sugary	athletes	breakfast	helmet	dogs

Across

2. Schools should not sell students __________ snacks.

sweet

6. Thanksgiving is the best __________ .

special day

9. Video __________ do not teach you anything.

something you play

10. You should not get __________ for helping out at home.

money for chores

Down

1. Cereal is a better __________ than eggs.

meal you eat in the morning

3. __________ are the most interesting of all zoo animals.

Animals with trunks

4. All children should do three hours of __________ every Saturday.

household tasks

5. Professional __________ make too much money.

people who play sports

7. Cats are better pets than __________.

canines

8. You should be able to choose whether to wear a bicycle __________ or not.

protection for your head

Name _______________   Date _______________   Helper _______________

Stating Opinions – Word Search

Instructions: Read the statements, and then circle the underlined words in the puzzle. Give your opinion for each statement.

```
M  D  T  M  J  H  H  F  T  H  D  K  H
K  A  J  E  O  G  O  B  Z  M  E  S  A
K  T  T  I  L  O  P  Y  G  G  W  R  L
L  E  W  H  T  E  G  H  C  V  O  W  L
Y  L  G  B  K  A  V  N  G  W  L  R  O
I  F  A  N  N  P  I  I  I  X  L  N  W
L  L  P  T  B  Y  Y  S  S  P  A  H  E
L  E  S  I  C  R  E  X  E  I  M  W  E
G  B  E  J  Y  N  I  J  J  G  O  A  N
I  S  W  M  O  T  H  N  Q  H  A  N  C
Y  X  H  H  B  X  Y  K  B  T  Y  A  R
Y  P  P  S  C  A  R  Y  V  E  Y  L  C
K  M  J  T  B  V  R  B  A  O  U  E  H
```

1. Only healthy treats should be given on <u>Halloween</u> — no candy.

2. Everyone on the team should get to play in the <u>football</u> game.

3. <u>Scary</u> movies are fun to watch.

4. Students should only watch one <u>television</u> program on school nights.

5. <u>Camping</u> is the best type of vacation.

6. <u>Math</u> is easier than social studies.

7. Skateboarding should only be <u>allowed</u> at skate parks.

8. Everyone should <u>exercise</u> two hours each day.

9. People should not <u>date</u> until they are 18 years old.

10. Students should not be allowed to have cell <u>phones</u>.

___________________ ___________________ ___________________
Name   Date   Helper

Stating Opinions – Draw a Picture

Instructions: Draw a picture in each box that goes with the statement below it. Give your opinion for each statement.

1.

Green is the best color for T-shirts.

2.

Rap music is better than rock music.

3.

Students should not be allowed to bring water bottles to school.

4.

Students should read two hours each night.

5.

Students should not be allowed to have cell phones.

6.

Cereal is a better breakfast than eggs.

Name   Date   Helper

Stating Opinions – Fact or Opinion?

Instructions: Read each statement. If it is a fact, write the word "fact" on the line. If it is an opinion, write the word "opinion." Tell whether or not you agree with each opinion.

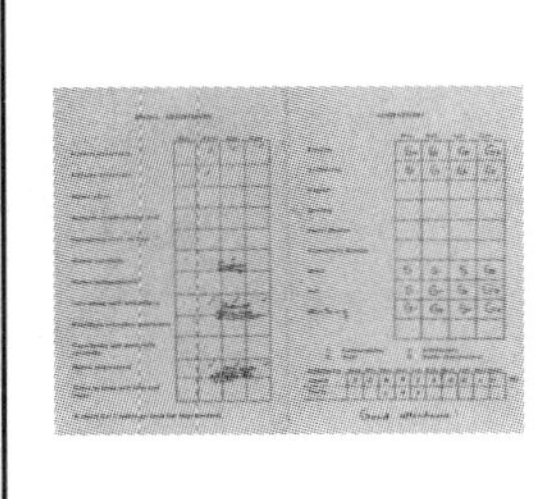

1. Math is a school subject.

   ____

6. Camping is the best type of vacation.

   ____

2. Rap music is better than rock music.

   ____

7. Professional athletes earn money to play sports.

   ____

3. Cats are better pets than dogs.

   ____

8. Schools should not sell students sugary snacks.

   ____

4. Elephants are very large animals.

   ____

9. Video games do not teach you anything.

   ____

5. Thanksgiving is a holiday.

   ____

10. Cereal is a breakfast food.

    ____

_______________________   _______________   _______________
        Name   Date   Helper

Stating Opinions – Fill It In

Instructions: Look at the photos. Then fill in the blanks with words from the Word Bank to complete the opinions. Tell whether or not you agree with each statement.

— Word Bank —

watch	hours	students	movies	babysitter	every
years	date			allowed	fun
old	candy	cards	healthy	program	parks

1. 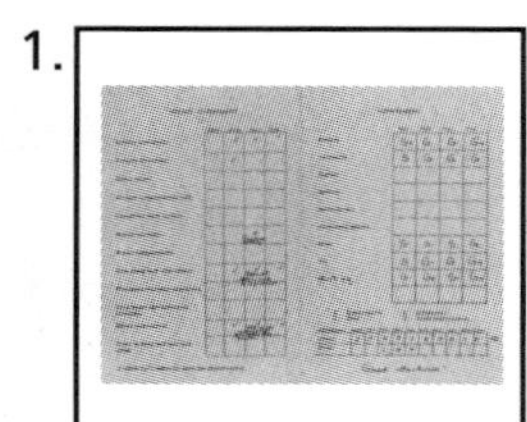 _______________ should get report _______________ every week.

5.  No one should _______________ until they are 18 years _______________.

2.  Students should only _______________ one television _______________ on school nights.

6.  Only _______________ treat should be given on Halloween — no _______________.

3.  Any child under 13 _______________ old should have a _______________.

7.  Scary _______________ are _______________ to watch.

4.  All children should do three _______________ of chores _______________ Saturday.

8.  Skateboarding should only be _______________ at skate _______________.

_______________ _______________ _______________
Name   Date   Helper

Stating Opinions – Answering Why Questions

Instructions: Read each statement. Answer each *Why* question by giving a good reason to support the opinion.

1. Everyone on the team should get to play in the football game.
   Why should everyone get to play?

2. Camping is the best type of vacation.
   Why is camping the best vacation?

3. Everyone should exercise two hours each day.
   Why should everyone exercise two hours each day?

4. Students should not be allowed to have cell phones.
   Why shouldn't students be allowed to have cell phones?

5. Cats are better pets than dogs.
   Why are cats better pets?

Name	Date	Helper

Stating Opinions – Your Own Opinion

Instructions: Look at the photos and subjects that go with them. Then write your opinion about each one.

1.  Driving age

2.  Math

3.  Chores

4.  Bicycle helmets

5.  Water bottles

Name	Date	Helper

Stating Opinions – Decode the Word

Instructions: Fill in each blank with the correct word. For help, use the Word Bank. Then transfer each letter that has a number under it to reveal the *Secret Word*. Give your opinion about each statement.

1.

Thanksgiving is the best

——— ——— ——— ——— ——— ——— ——— ——— .
                               ④

Word Bank

holiday
Halloween
elephants
breakfast
color

4.
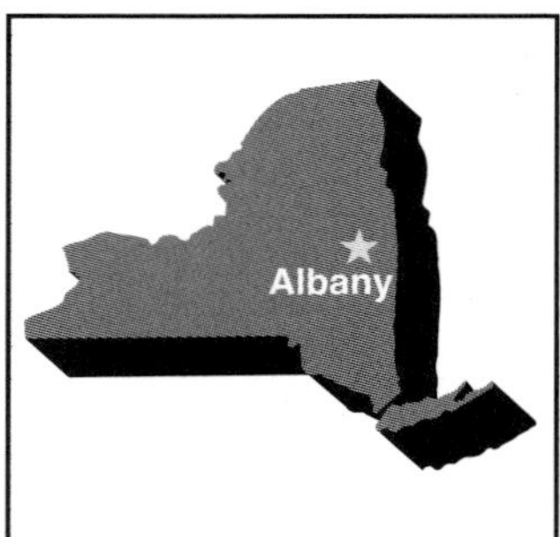

Only healthy treats should be given on

——— ——— ——— ——— ——— ——— ——— ——— ———
                ③   ②
— no candy.

2.

——— ——— ——— ——— ——— ——— ——— ——— ———
                   ①

are the most interesting of all zoo animals.

5.

Green is the best

——— ——— ——— ——— ——— for T-shirts.
     ⑤   ⑥

3.

Cereal is a better

——— ——— ——— ——— ——— ——— ——— ——— ———
              ⑦

than eggs.

What state is this?

——— ——— ——— ——— ——— ——— ———
 1   2   3   4   5   6   7

Secret Word

—————————————————— —————————— ——————————————
       Name   Date   Helper

Stating Opinions – Do You Agree or Disagree?

Instructions: Read each statement. If you agree with the opinion, color the *happy* face. If you disagree with the opinion, color the *sad* face. Tell why you agree or disagree with each statement.

1. Everyone should go to bed at 8:00 p.m. 

2. Any child under 13 years old should have a babysitter. 

3. You should be able to choose whether you wear a bicycle helmet or not. 

4. You should not get an allowance for helping out at home. 

5. Students should read two hours each night. 

6. All students should take cell phones to school. 

7. Everyone on the team should get to play in the football game. 

8. Green is the best color for T-shirts. 

Name	Date	Helper

Stating Opinions – Fact or Opinion in School

Instructions: Read the statements in the schoolhouse. Color all the facts *red*. Color all the opinions *yellow*.

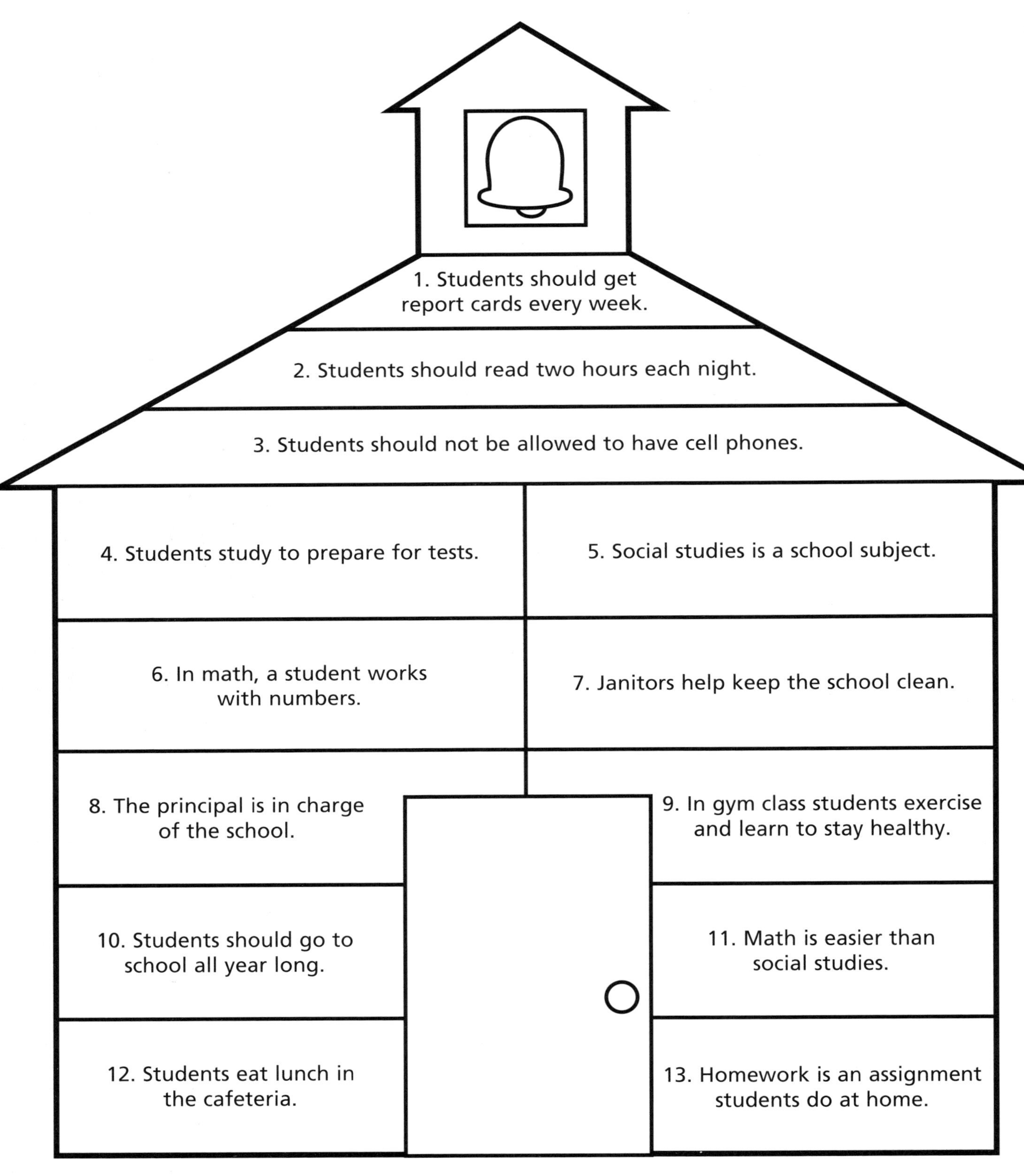

Name

Date

Helper

Stating Opinions – What Is It?

Instructions: Look at each photo and read the statement that goes with it. Then write a definition for the word in *italics*. Tell whether you agree or disagree with the statement.

1. All students should take cell phones to *school*.

   Definition: _______________________________

   ____

   ____

2. Any child under 13 years old should have a *babysitter*.

   Definition: _______________________________

   ____

   ____

3. You should not get an *allowance* for helping out at home.

   Definition: _______________________________

   ____

   ____

4. You should be able to choose whether you wear a bicycle *helmet* or not.

   Definition: _______________________________

   ____

   ____

5. *Elephants* are the most interesting of all zoo animals.

   Definition: _______________________________

   ____

   ____

Name	Date	Helper

Stating Opinions – Write Another Opinion

Instructions: Look at each photo and read the statement that goes with it. Then write another opinion about the topic.

1. Rap music is better rock music.

____

____

____

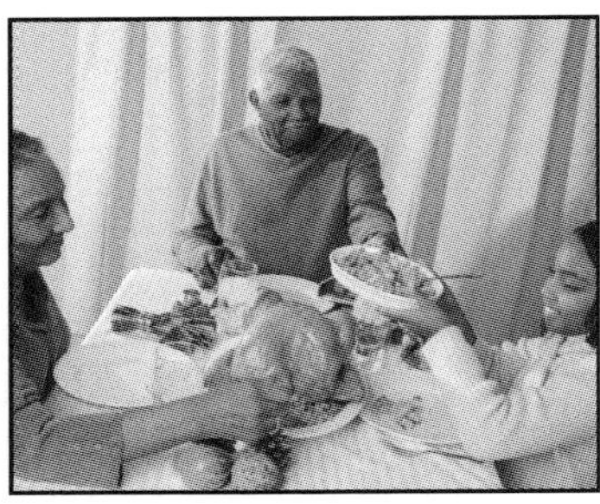

2. Thanksgiving is the best holiday.

____

____

____

3. Green is the best color for T-shirts.

____

____

____

4. Professional athletes make too much money.

____

____

____

5. People should be able to drive when they are fourteen years old.

____

____

____

______________________   ______________________   ______________________
Name   Date   Helper

Intonation & Body Language – Match It Up

Instructions: Read each question below. Under each photo write the number of the question that matches it. Then circle the words in the questions that gave you clues.

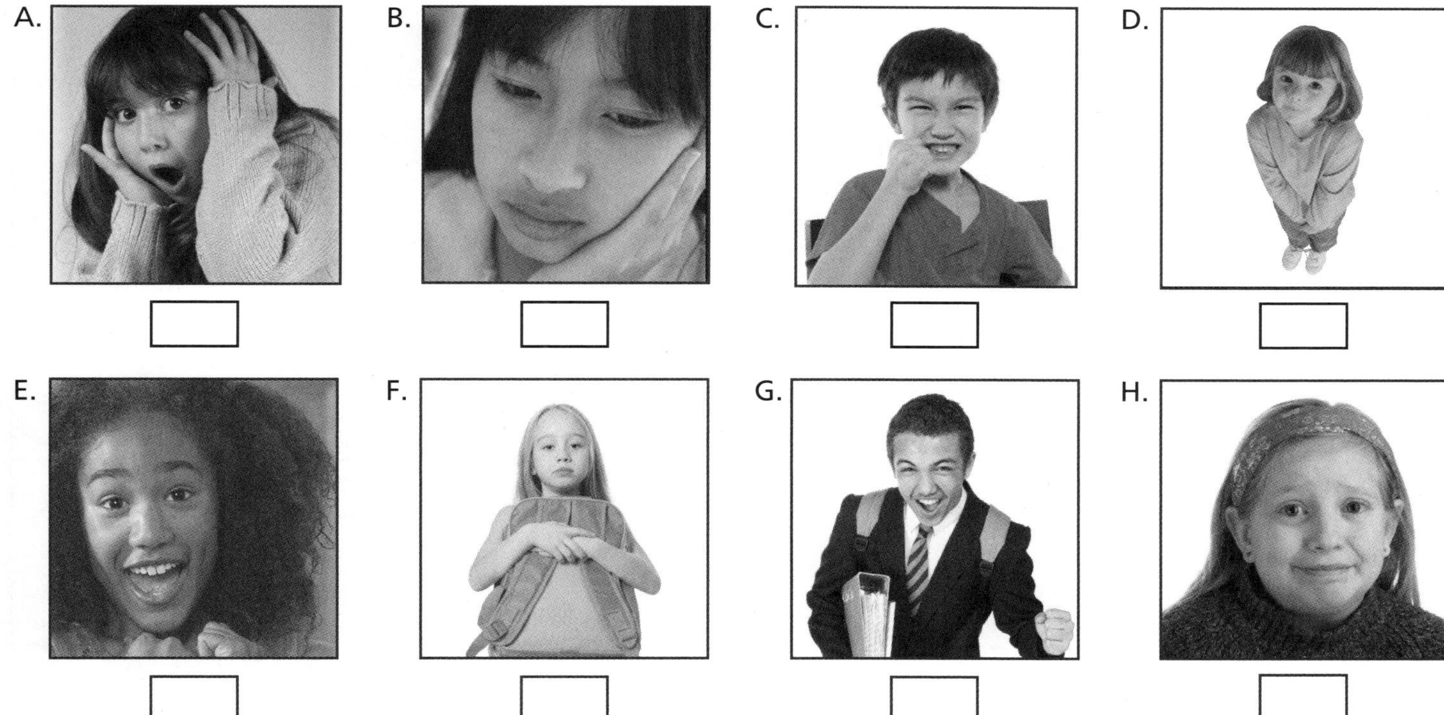

A.   B.   C.   D.

E.   F.   G.   H.

1. How would you look if you met your favorite TV star?

2. How would you look if you couldn't get your video game to work?

3. How would you look if you wanted your parents to buy you a puppy?

4. How would you look if your best friend moved away?

5. How would you look if you heard a scary noise?

6. How would you look if you dropped your tray in the cafeteria?

7. How would you look if you got straight A's on your report card?

8. How would you look if you were waiting half an hour for your ride?

_________________________ _______________ _________________________
Name   Date   Helper

Intonation & Body Language – Memory Game

Instructions: Cut out the cards. Shuffle the statement cards and photo-emotion cards and place them facedown. Player One chooses two cards. If the statement card matches the photo-emotion card, player keeps the pair and reads the statement using the correct intonation. Player with the most matches is the winner. There may be more than one correct answer for the statements.

Your room is always a mess. Now, you must stay in and clean it!	angry	I was waiting for half an hour, and you didn't show up.	upset
It snowed last night, so we don't have school today!	excited	May I please go to the movies? I've finished my homework.	persuasive
I'm sorry. I didn't mean to spill the paint.	apologetic	My team lost in overtime.	sad
Dad, you forgot to give me lunch money.	frustrated	We do not have any homework tonight!	surprised

Name   Date   Helper

Intonation & Body Language – Where Was the Photo Taken?

Instructions: Read each situation and find the photo on the map that matches it. Then write the name of the city where the photo was taken. For each situation, show or tell how you would feel.

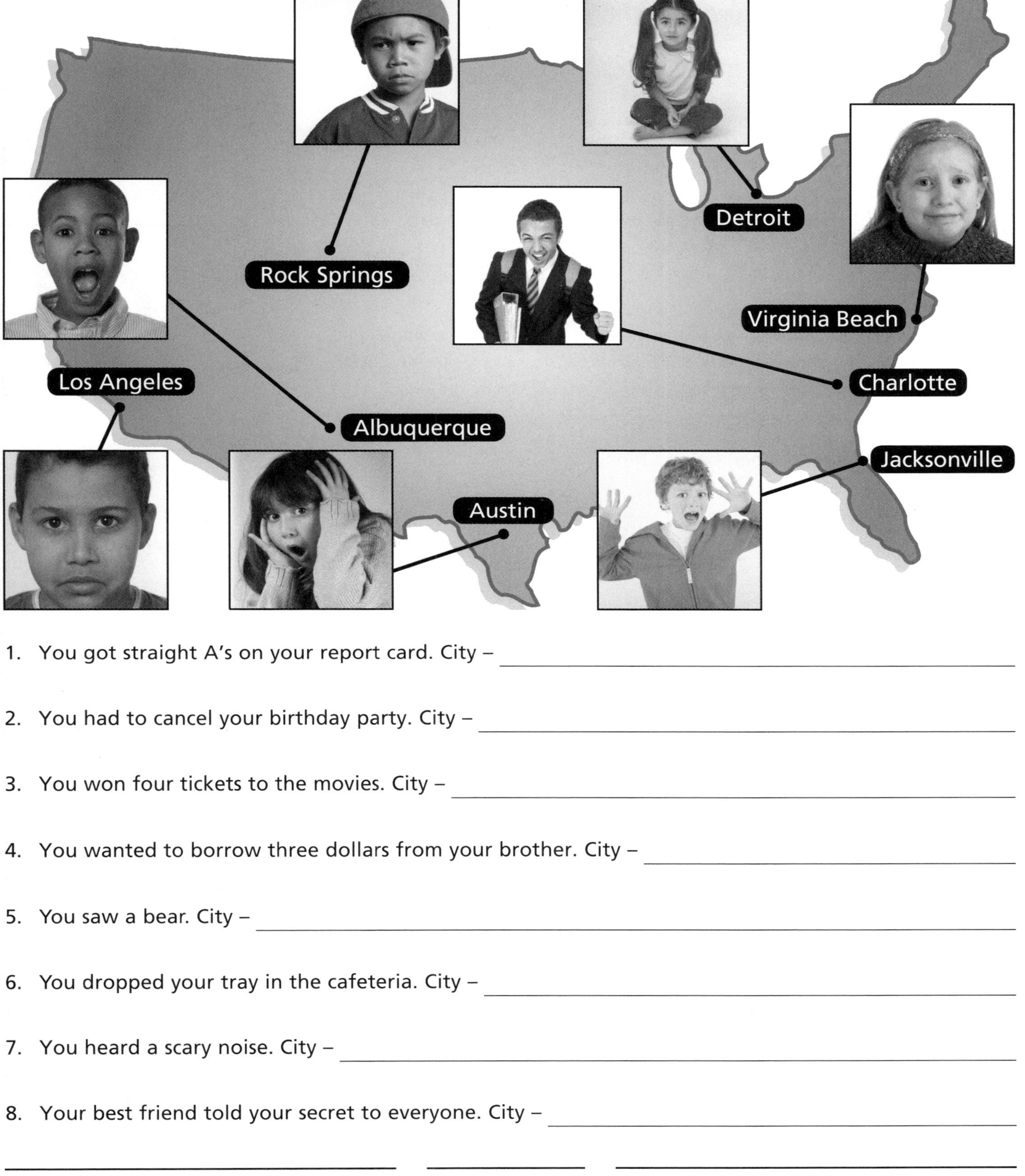

1. You got straight A's on your report card. City – _______________________________

2. You had to cancel your birthday party. City – _______________________________

3. You won four tickets to the movies. City – _______________________________

4. You wanted to borrow three dollars from your brother. City – _______________________________

5. You saw a bear. City – _______________________________

6. You dropped your tray in the cafeteria. City – _______________________________

7. You heard a scary noise. City – _______________________________

8. Your best friend told your secret to everyone. City – _______________________________

_______________________   _______________   _______________________
          Name   Date   Helper

Intonation & Body Language – The Best Intonation

Instructions: Read each sentence. Then circle the best intonation that you would use to say the sentence. Say the sentences aloud with the correct intonations.

1. I have three tests tomorrow.

   A. excited

   B. worried

   C. happy

2. I can't find my new bracelet.

   A. surprised

   B. pleasant

   C. upset

3. I got a letter from my pen pal in China.

   A. excited

   B. angry

   C. annoyed

4. Grandma is in the hospital.

   A. excited

   B. sad

   C. mad

5. Take the garbage out now, please!

   A. nervous

   B. happy

   C. annoyed

___________________________   ___________________   ___________________________
Name   Date   Helper

Intonation & Body Language – Guess the Expression

Instructions: To assemble the cube, cut on the dotted lines. Fold on the solid lines and glue/tape as indicated. To play, roll the cube. Player One reads the situation on the top side of the cube with the appropriate intonation. Other players guess what intonation Player One is using.

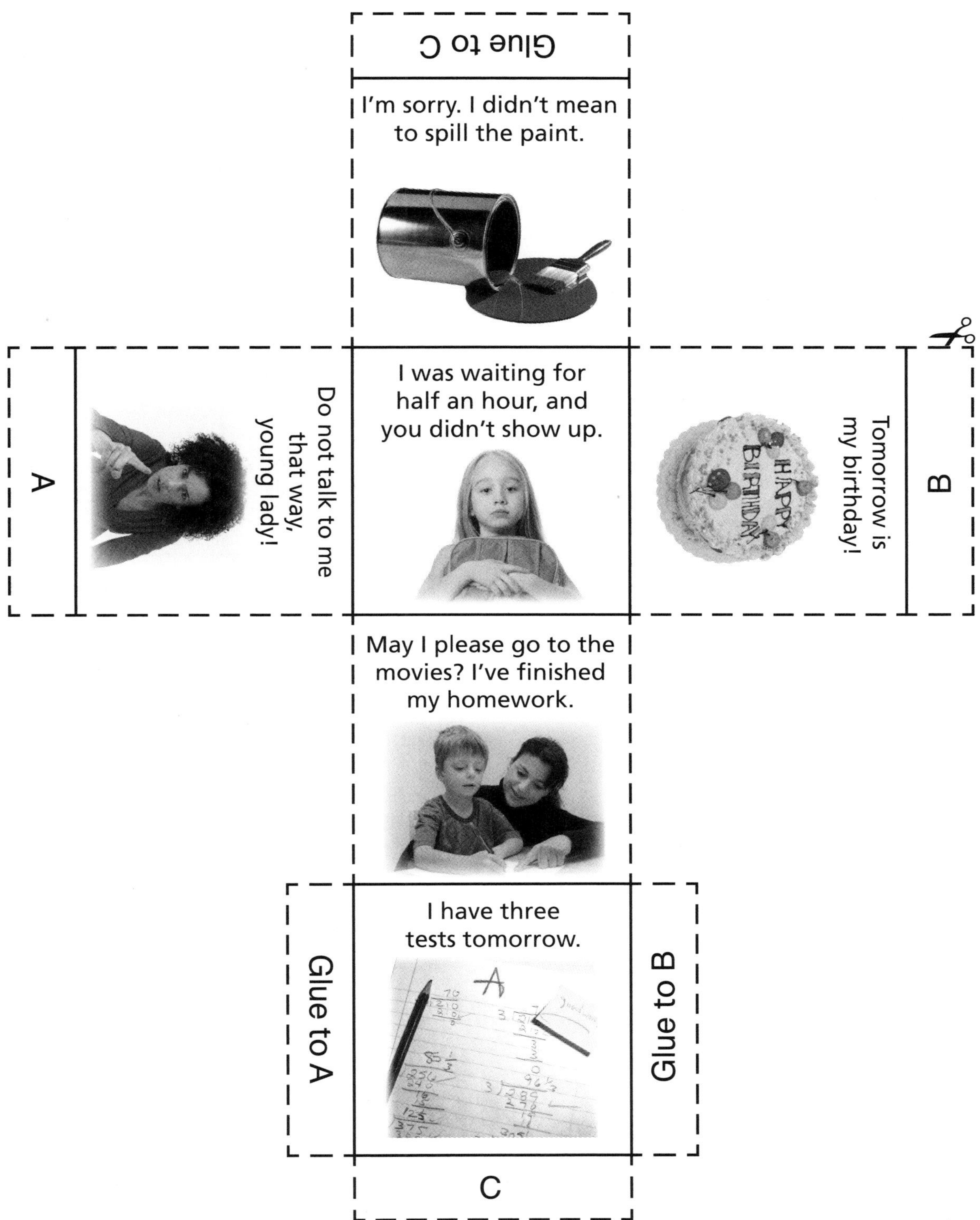

Name	Date	Helper

Intonation & Body Language – Which Intonation?

Instructions: Cut out the photos at the bottom of the page. Then glue/tape each photo next to the sentence that goes with it. Read each sentence with the appropriate intonation.

1. Dad, you forgot to give me lunch money.

4. It snowed last night, so we don't have school today!

2. My team lost in overtime.

5. Do not talk to me that way, young lady!

3. I got a letter from my pen pal in China.

6. Grandma is in the hospital.

_________________ _________________ _________________
Name   Date   Helper

Intonation & Body Language – Half-Match

Instructions: Cut out the photos/intonations at the bottom of the page. Then glue/tape them under the matching photos/situations. Say the sentences using the given intonation.

1.  Take out the garbage now, please!

2. 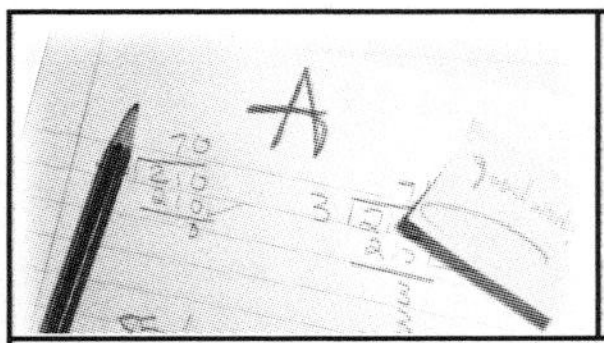 I have three tests tomorrow.

3.  May I please go to the movies? I've finished my homework.

4. 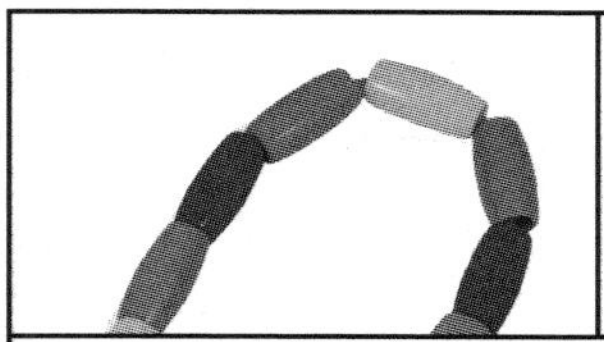 I can't find my new bracelet.

5.  Tomorrow is my birthday!

6.  I'm sorry. I didn't mean to spill the paint.

___________ Name   ___________ Date   ___________ Helper

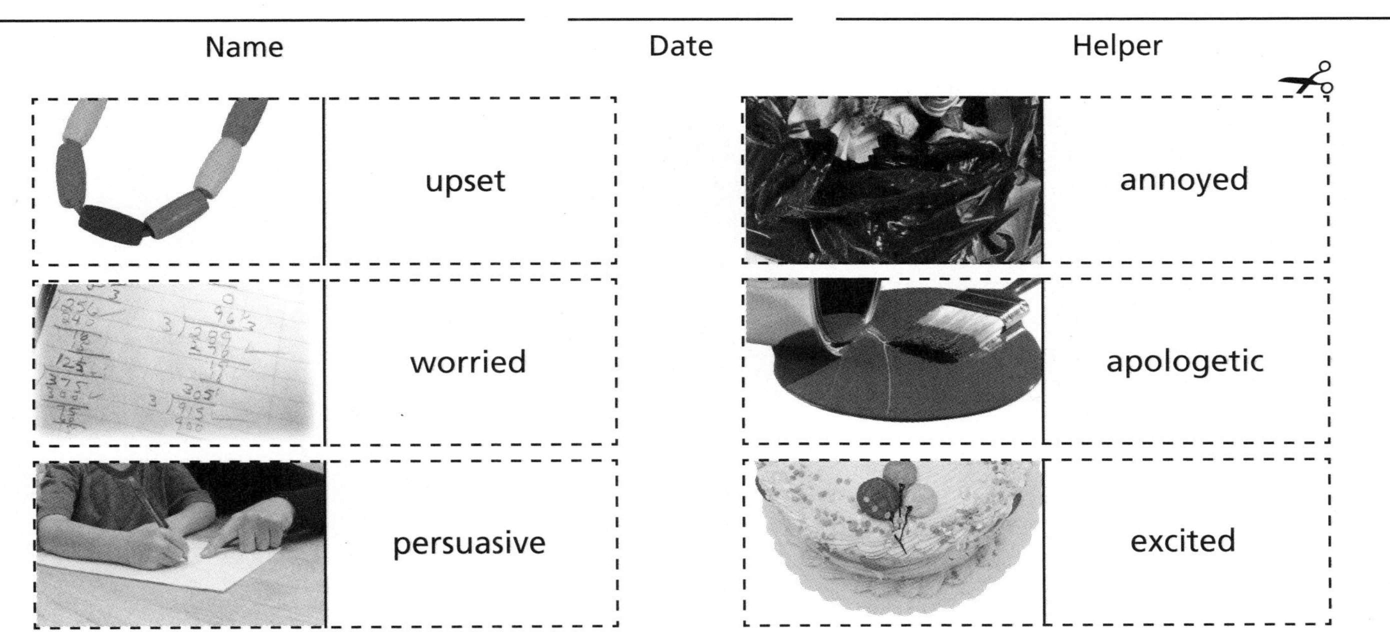

upset

worried

persuasive

annoyed

apologetic

excited

Intonation & Body Language – Act It Out

Instructions: Cut out the cards. Shuffle and place all cards facedown. Player One chooses a card and acts out the situation. Other players try to guess the situation. Play continues in turn.

You dropped your tray in the cafeteria. 	You got straight A's on your report card. 	You couldn't get your video game to work. 
You were late for your soccer game. 	You met your favorite TV star. 	You heard a scary noise. 
You broke your mom's new cell phone. 	You wanted your parents to buy you a puppy. 	Your parents gave you a new bike for your birthday. 

____________________ ____________________ ____________________
Name Date Helper

Intonation & Body Language – Crossword

Instructions: Read each situation. Then find the word in the Word Bank that describes how someone would look in that situation.

Word Bank

proud	embarrassed	sad	sorry	disappointed
scared	surprised	angry	excited	persuasive

Across

3. You saw a bear.
6. You got straight *A*'s on your report card.
7. You broke your mom's new cell phone.
8. Your parents gave you a new bike for your birthday.
10. You dropped your tray in the cafeteria.

Down

1. You had to cancel your birthday party.
2. You wanted your parents to buy you a puppy.
4. Your best friend told your secret to everyone.
5. You met your favorite TV star.
9. Your best friend moved away.

___________________   ___________   ___________________
Name   Date   Helper

Intonation & Body Language – Word Search

Instructions: Read the sentences below using an appropriate intonation. Then circle the intonation words in the puzzle. For help, use the Word Bank. (There may be more than one correct intonation.)

Word Bank

| annoyed | excited | sad | persuasive | angry |
| apologetic | surprised | upset | mad | worried |

```
N  M  A  P  S  K  D  W  T  E  C  A  Q
O  O  N  N  N  Z  O  K  V  X  I  A  H
A  K  W  M  N  R  J  I  P  C  T  S  S
Q  Y  I  O  R  O  S  N  L  I  E  O  A
Q  X  R  I  C  A  Y  W  J  T  G  H  G
Q  M  E  G  U  V  M  E  Y  E  O  Y  U
V  D  K  S  N  F  B  T  D  D  L  L  U
R  H  R  W  R  A  S  G  Z  P  O  L  X
U  E  A  S  U  P  S  O  R  D  P  R  D
P  T  E  S  P  U  J  F  D  A  A  A  I
S  U  R  P  R  I  S  E  D  S  M  P  C
W  E  E  I  R  Q  K  F  N  R  V  K  U
X  I  R  Y  T  D  Q  I  A  I  F  F  Q
```

1. May I please go to the movies? I've finished my homework.

2. We do not have any homework tonight!

3. It snowed last night, so we don't have school today!

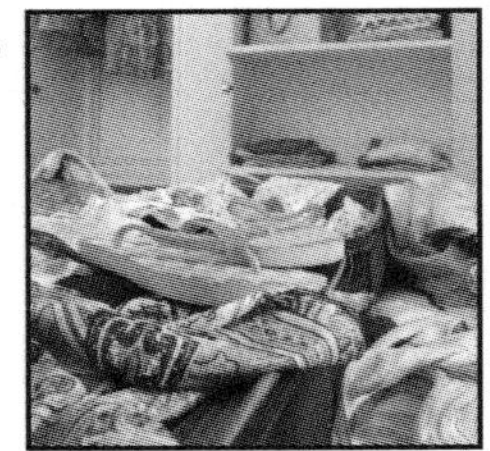

4. Your room is always a mess. Now, you must stay in and clean it!

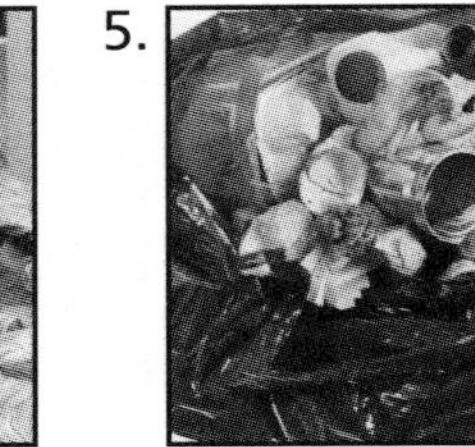

5. Take the garbage out now, please!

6. I have three tests tomorrow.

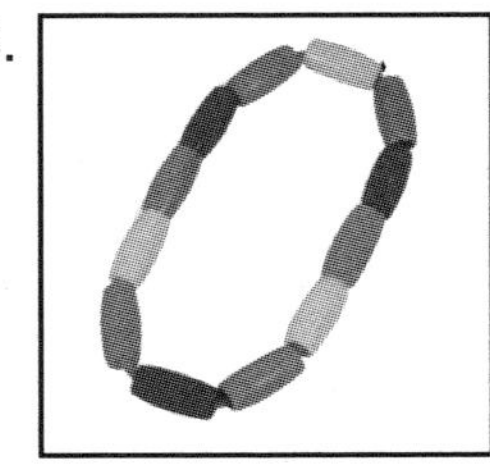

7.  Do not talk to me that way, young lady!

8. I can't find my new bracelet.

9. My team lost in overtime.

10. I'm sorry. I didn't mean to spill the paint.

___________________________ ______________ ___________________
Name   Date   Helper

Intonation & Body Language – Draw a Picture

Instructions: Draw a picture in each box that answers the question below it.

1.

How would you look if you couldn't get your video game to work?

2.

How would you look if you heard a scary noise?

3.

How would you look if you met your favorite TV star?

4.

How would you look if your parents gave you a new bike for your birthday?

5.

How would you look if you wanted your parents to buy you a puppy?

6.

How would you look if you broke your mom's new cell phone?

Name　　　　Date　　　　Helper

Intonation & Body Language – Five Word Association

Instructions: Write three different feelings that could be associated with each photo.

A.

1. _______________________
2. _______________________
3. _______________________

B.

1. _______________________
2. _______________________
3. _______________________

C.

1. _______________________
2. _______________________
3. _______________________

D.

1. _______________________
2. _______________________
3. _______________________

E.

1. _______________________
2. _______________________
3. _______________________

F.

1. _______________________
2. _______________________
3. _______________________

G.

1. _______________________
2. _______________________
3. _______________________

H.

1. _______________________
2. _______________________
3. _______________________

I.

1. _______________________
2. _______________________
3. _______________________

_______________________ _______________________ _______________________
Name   Date   Helper

Intonation & Body Language – Fill It In

Instructions: Look at the photos. Then fill in the blanks with words from the Word Bank to complete the sentences.

<table>
<tr><td colspan="6" align="center">— Word Bank —</td></tr>
<tr><td>star</td><td>bear</td><td>birthday</td><td>sad</td><td>surprised</td><td>cafeteria</td></tr>
<tr><td>friend</td><td>frustrated</td><td>embarrassed</td><td>parents</td><td>disappointed</td><td>excited</td></tr>
<tr><td>happy</td><td>video</td><td></td><td></td><td>movies</td><td>scared</td></tr>
</table>

1. 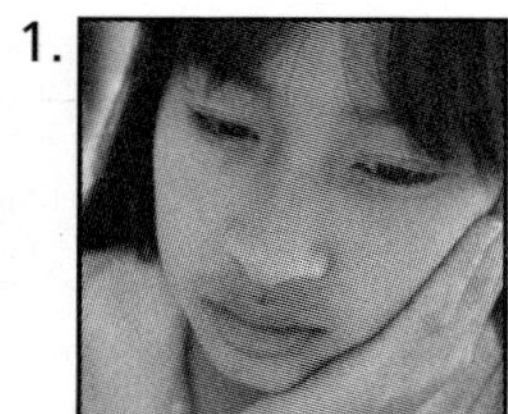 If your best _______________ moved away, you would look _______________.

5. 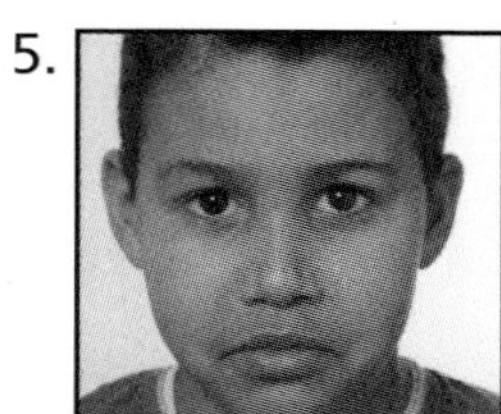 If you had to cancel your _______________ party, you would look _______________.

2.  If you couldn't get your _______________, game to work, you would look _______________.

6.  If you saw a _______________ you would look _______________.

3. 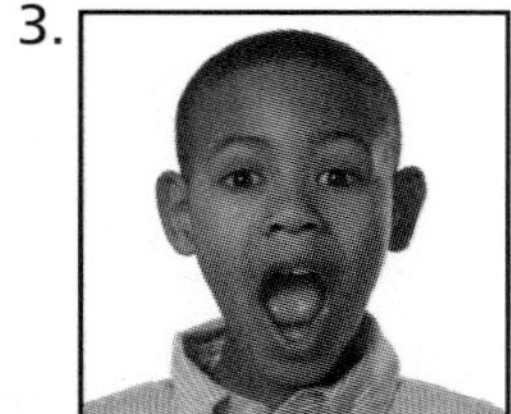 If you won four tickets to the _______________ you would look _______________.

7.  If you met your favorite TV _______________ you would look _______________.

4.  If you dropped your tray in the _______________ you would look _______________.

8.  If your _______________ gave you a new bike for your birthday, you would look _______________.

_______________   _______________   _______________
Name   Date   Helper

Intonation & Body Language – Answering Why Questions

Instructions: Look at the photos and then answer the *Why* questions.

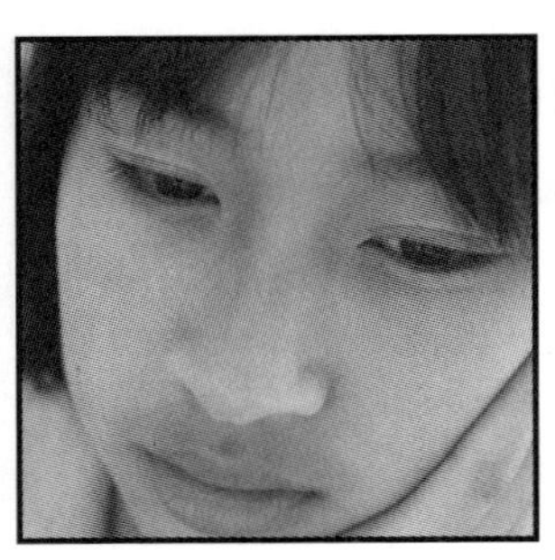

1. Why would you look sad if your best friend moved away?

____

____

____

2. Why would you look embarrassed if you dropped your tray in the cafeteria?

____

____

____

3. Why would you look angry if your best friend told your secret to everyone?

____

____

____

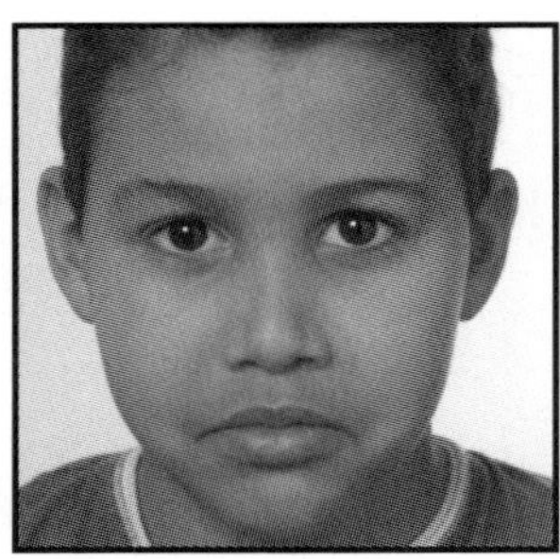

4. Why would you look disappointed if you had to cancel your birthday party?

____

____

____

5. Why would you look upset if you broke your mom's new cell phone?

____

____

____

Name   Date   Helper

Intonation & Body Language – Ask a Question

Instructions: Look at each photo and read the answer. Then write a question you could ask to get that answer.

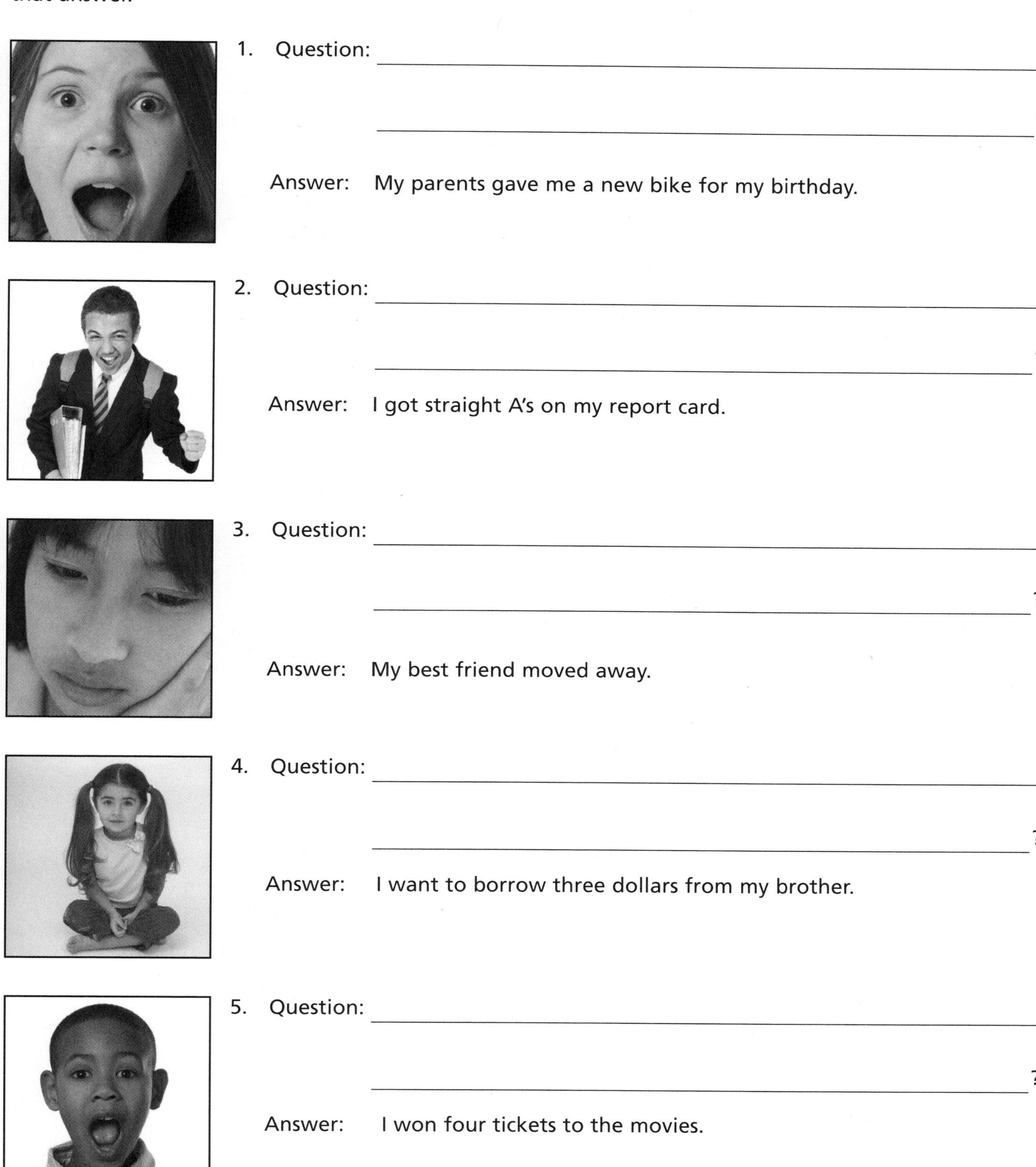

1. Question: ____

   ____ ?

   Answer: My parents gave me a new bike for my birthday.

2. Question: ____

   ____ ?

   Answer: I got straight A's on my report card.

3. Question: ____

   ____ ?

   Answer: My best friend moved away.

4. Question: ____

   ____ ?

   Answer: I want to borrow three dollars from my brother.

5. Question: ____

   ____ ?

   Answer: I won four tickets to the movies.

Name	Date	Helper

Intonation & Body Language – Decode the Word

Instructions: Fill in each blank with the correct word. For help, use the Word Bank. Then transfer each letter that has a number under it to reveal the *Secret Word*.

_______ **Word Bank** _______

excited	disappointed	angry
upset		embarrassed

1. 

If you broke your mom's new cell phone, you would look

___ ___ ___ ___ ___.
　　　⑤

2. 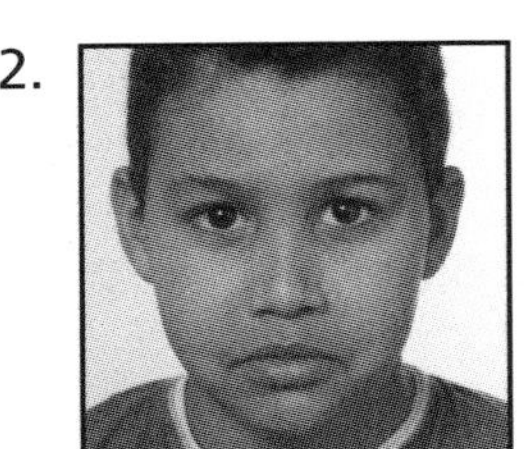

If you had to cancel your birthday party, you would look

___ ___ ___ ___ ___ ___ ___ ___ ___ ___ ___ ___.
　　　④

3.  

If you dropped your tray in the cafeteria, you would look

___ ___ ___ ___ ___ ___ ___ ___ ___ ___ ___.
　①

4.

If your best friend told your secret to everyone, you would look

___ ___ ___ ___ ___.
　　　②

5. 

If you met your favorite TV star, you would look

___ ___ ___ ___ ___ ___ ___.
　　　③

What state is this?

___ ___ ___ ___ ___
 1   2   3   4   5
Secret Word

___________________ ___________________ ___________________
　　　　Name　　　　　　　　　　Date　　　　　　　　　　Helper

Intonation & Body Language – Right or Wrong Intonation?

Instructions: Read each situation. If the intonation is right, color the *happy* face. If the intonation is wrong, color the *sad* face. For every sad face, give a correct intonation. Say each sentence using an appropriate intonation.

1. Tomorrow is my birthday!

   Intonation: excited

2. Your room is always a mess. Now, you must stay in and clean it!

   Intonation: happy

3. Grandma is in the hospital.

   Intonation: upset

4. We do not have any homework tonight!

   Intonation: sad

5. I was waiting for half an hour, and you didn't show up.

   Intonation: annoyed

6. My team lost in overtime.

   Intonation: persuasive

7. I got a letter from my pen pal in China.

   Intonation: frustrated

8. I have three tests tomorrow.

   Intonation: worried

Name   Date   Helper

Intonation & Body Language – Story Writer

Instructions: Look at the photos and then write a short story about each one. In each story, tell why the person is using the body language he/she is using and what his/her intonation would be.

1.

2.

3.

Name   Date   Helper

Intonation & Body Language – What Is It?

Instructions: Look at each photo, and using the appropriate intonation, read the statement that goes with it. Then write a definition for the word in *italics*.

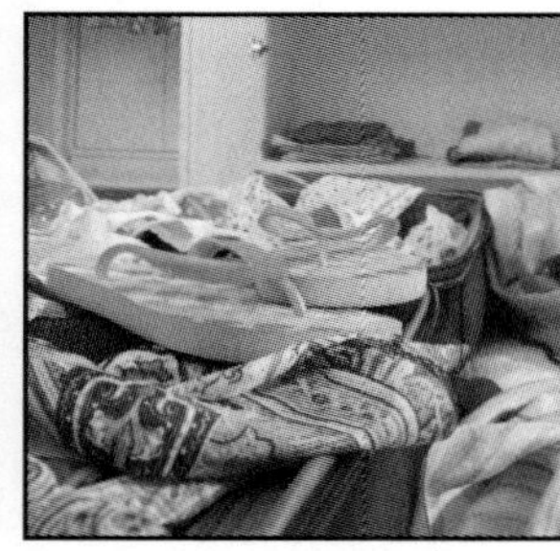

1. Your room is always a *mess*. Now, you must stay in and clean it!

   Definition: ____

   ____

   ____

2. Tomorrow is my *birthday*!

   Definition: ____

   ____

   ____

3. Grandma is in the *hospital*.

   Definition: ____

   ____

   ____

4. My team lost in *overtime*.

   Definition: ____

   ____

   ____

5. I got a letter from my *pen pal* in China.

   Definition: ____

   ____

   ____

___________________________ ___________ ___________________________
Name   Date   Helper

Intonation & Body Language – Two Ways to Say It

Instructions: Look at each photo and the sentence(s) below it. Read the sentence(s) using two different intonations. Write the intonation words on the lines.

1.

I have three
tests tomorrow.

____

____

2.
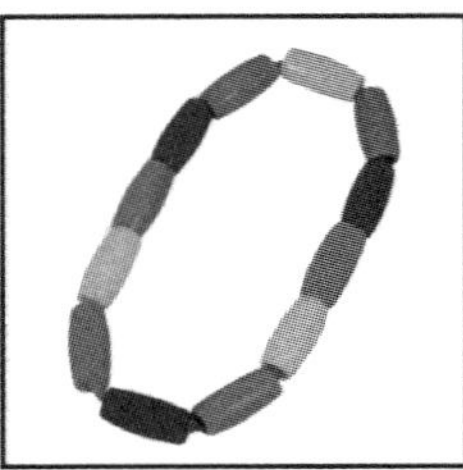
I can't find my
new bracelet.

____

____

3.

Take the garbage
out now, please!

____

____

4.

I'm sorry. I didn't mean
to spill the paint.

____

____

5.

I was waiting for half an
hour, and you didn't show up.

____

____

6.
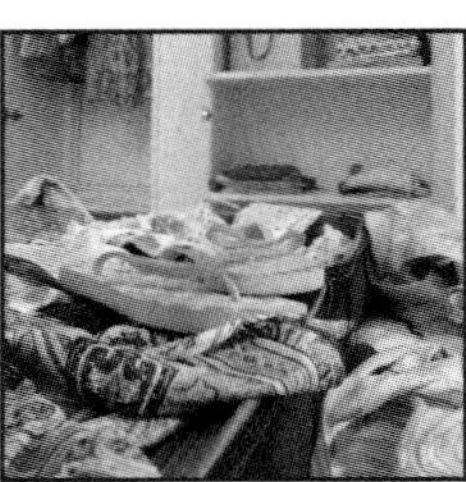
Your room is always a mess.
Now, you must stay in and clean it!

____

____

7.

We do not have any
homework tonight!

____

____

8.

May I please go to the movies?
I've finished my homework.

____

____

9.

Grandma is in
the hospital.

____

____

Name _______________________ Date _______________________ Helper _______________________

Social Encouragement – Match It Up

Instructions: Read each situation below. Under each photo write the number of the situation that matches it. Tell what you could say or do to make each person feel better.

A.

B.

C.

D.

E.

F.

G.

H.

1. Your friend feels hurt because she did not get an invitation to your classmate's party.

____

2. You see a younger student in the hallway who is lost and scared.

____

3. Your brother has a black eye and does not want to go to school.

____

4. Mary is angry because her parents will not let her go to the dance.

____

5. During a sleepover, Sue spills grape juice on your mom's white couch, and she begins to cry.

____

6. Sarah sat on a cupcake and ruined her new dress.

____

7. Bobby is feeling sad because he did not make the baseball team.

____

8. Grandpa cannot get out of bed because he hurt his back.

____

Name	Date	Helper

Social Encouragement – Memory Game

Instructions: Cut out the cards. Shuffle and place all cards facedown. Player One chooses two cards to try to match the situation card with the corresponding photo. When a player makes a match, he/she tells what to say or do to make the person described on the card feel better. Player Two follows in turn. The player with the most matches wins.

Charlie's name is not on the list for the all-star basketball team, and his feelings are hurt.

Michael is frustrated because he doesn't understand his homework.

The football players are discouraged because their team lost every game.

Your friend got braces, and she does not like the way she looks.

Grandma is feeling lonely because she lives by herself.

Wayne is worried about getting a flu shot this afternoon.

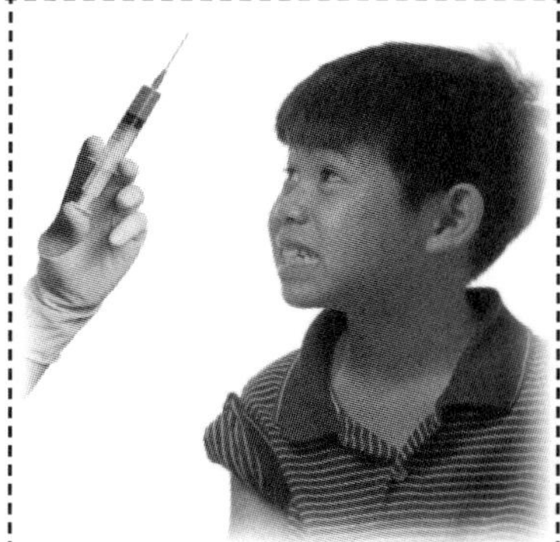

Mom is annoyed because there are piles of dirty dishes in the sink.

Your baby brother is crying because his tower of blocks keeps falling over.

______________________   ______________________   ______________________
Name   Date   Helper

Social Encouragement – Where Was the Photo Taken?

Instructions: Read each situation and find the photo on the map that matches it. Then write the name of the city where the photo was taken. Tell what you could say or do to make each person feel better.

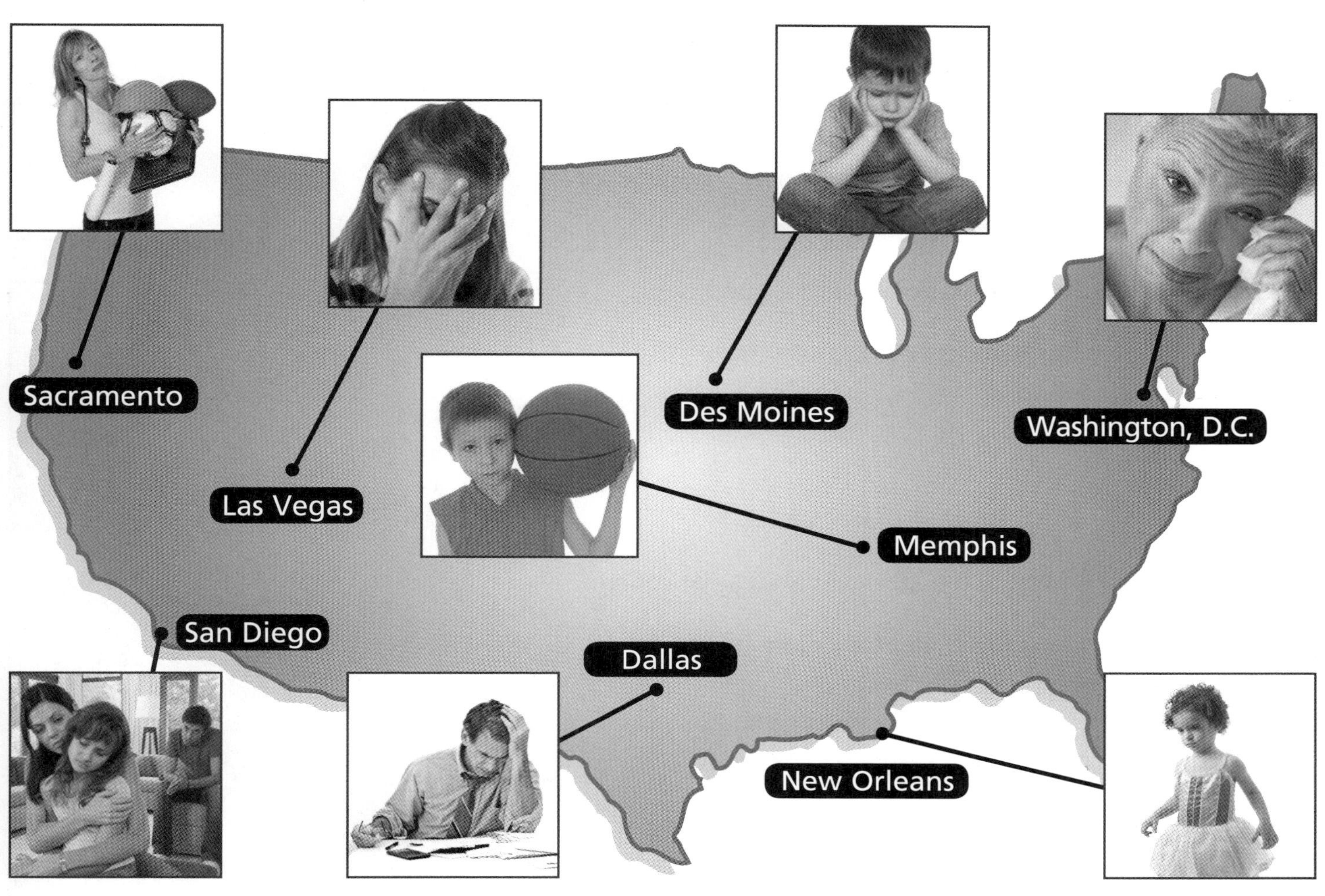

1. Your friend has a red rash on her face, and she does not want anyone to notice. City – _______________

2. Wes misses an easy basket, and his team loses the game. City – _______________

3. Grandma is feeling lonely because she lives by herself. City – _______________

4. Jack's dog is lost, and he has not been able to find him. City – _______________

5. Dad is worried about paying bills. City – _______________

6. Amanda does the wrong steps in the dance recital and is embarrassed. City – _______________

7. Mom is upset because she has too much work to do. City – _______________

8. Katie is sad because her parents are separating. City – _______________

_______________________   _______________   _______________
Name   Date   Helper

Social Encouragement – The Best Way

Instructions: Read each situation below. Then circle the best way to make the person feel better.

1. Kathy must start speech therapy, and she does not want to go.

    A. Tell her to stop being a baby.
    B. Introduce her to a friend who goes to speech therapy who can tell her why it is fun.
    C. Tell her she will have to do a lot of speech homework.

2. You can tell your teacher is not having a good day.

    A. Try extra hard to behave and pay attention.
    B. Talk to your friend about your new video game.
    C. Stare out the window.

3. Your neighbor is missing her son who is away at college.

    A. Tell her that her son is mean for going away.
    B. Remind her every day that her son is away.
    C. Offer to help her bake cookies to send to her son.

4. Your sister is worried about her friend who is sick.

    A. Tell your sister to stop thinking about her friend.
    B. Go with your sister to visit her friend.
    C. Tell your sister she worries too much.

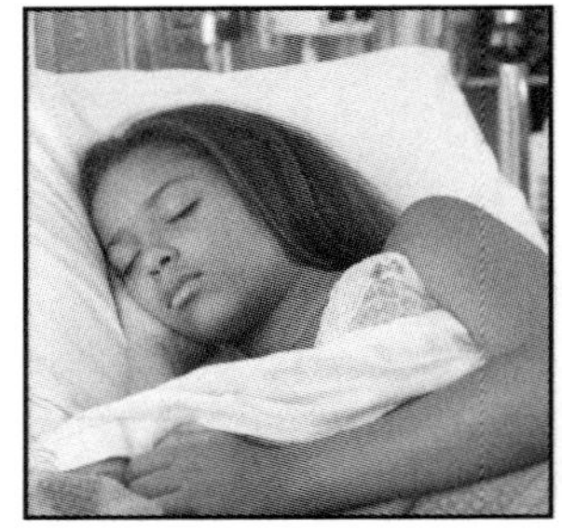

5. Brianna's mom is making her wear her hair in curls for her school picture, and she is embarrassed.

    A. Tell her you think her hair always looks nice, even when it is curly.
    B. Tell her she looks better with straight hair.
    C. Tell her she should tell her mom, "No!"

_______________________________ ________________ _______________________________
Name   Date   Helper

Social Encouragement – What Would You Say or Do?

Instructions: To assemble the cube, cut on the dotted lines. Fold on the solid lines and glue/tape as indicated. To play, roll the cube. Read the situation on the top side of the cube. Tell what you could say or do to make the person feel better.

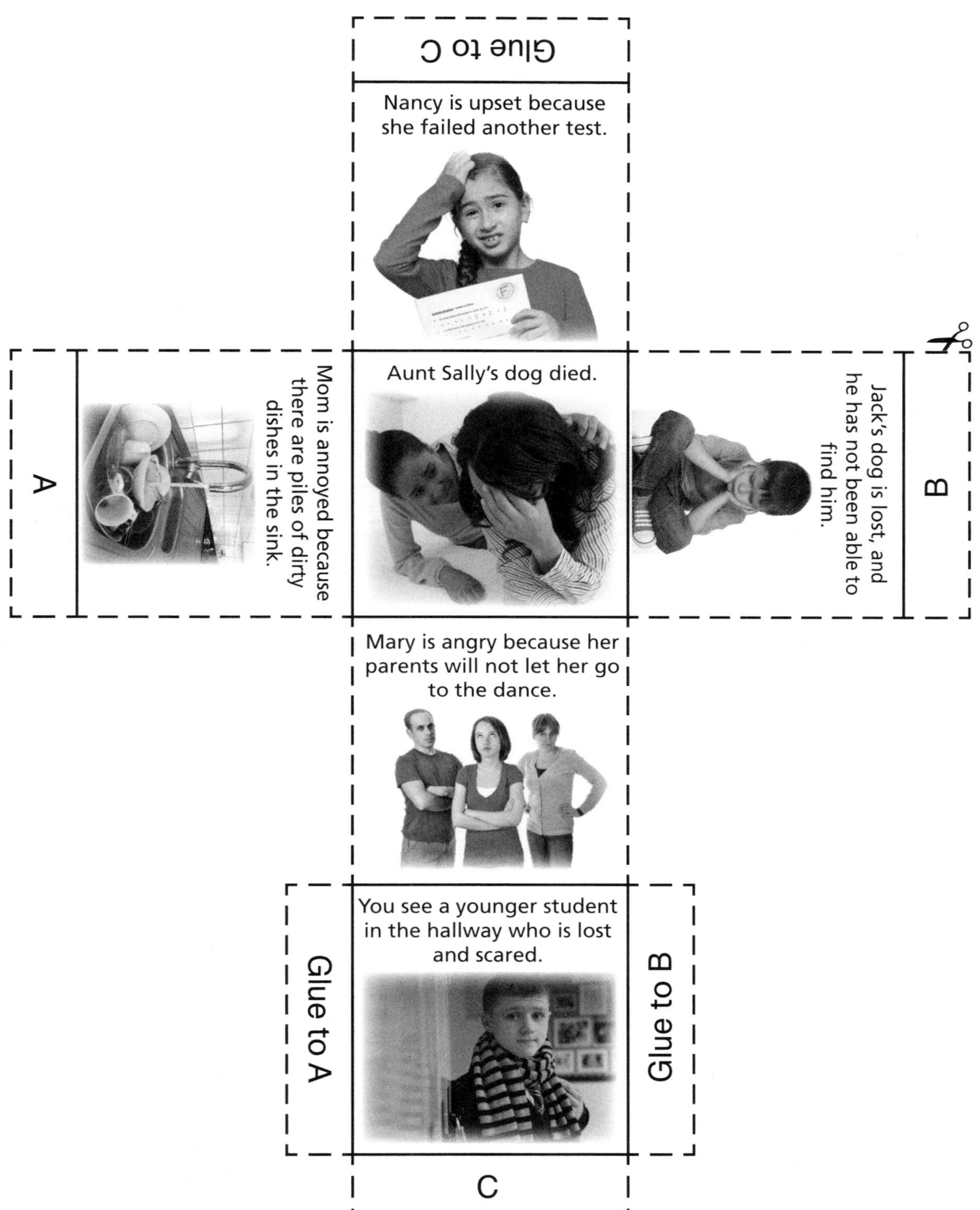

______________________ ______________________ ______________________
Name   Date   Helper

Social Encouragement – Match the Photo

Instructions: Cut out the photos at the bottom of the page. Then glue/tape each photo next to the situation that goes with it. Tell what you could say or do to help the person.

1. Michael is frustrated because he doesn't understand his homework.

2. Your brother has a black eye and does not want to go to school.

3. Your baby brother is crying because his tower of blocks keeps falling over.

4. You can tell your teacher is not having a good day.

5. Dad is worried about paying bills.

6. Bobby is feeling sad because he did not make the baseball team.

Name

Date

Helper

Social Encouragement – Half-Match

Instructions: Cut out the photos/sentences of encouragement at the bottom of the page. Then glue/tape them under the matching photos/situations.

1.  Mom is upset because she has too much work to do.

2.  Sarah sat on a cupcake and ruined her new dress.

3. 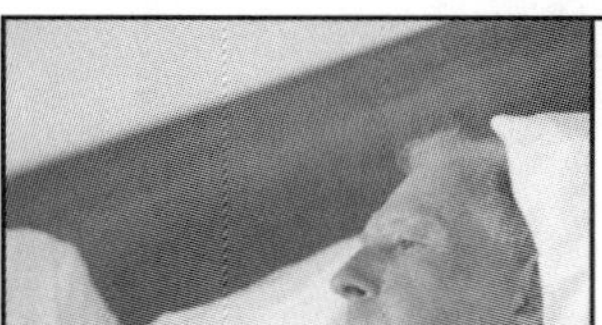 Grandpa cannot get out of bed because he hurt his back.

4. 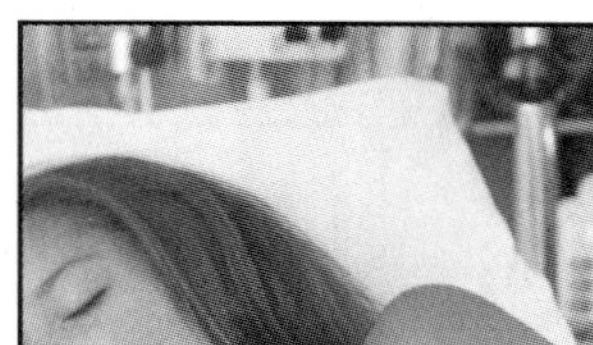 Your sister is worried about her friend who is sick.

5.  Charlie's name is not on the list for the all-star basketball team, and his feelings are hurt.

6. 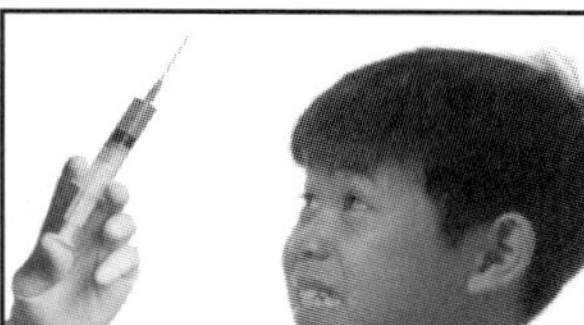 Wayne is worried about getting a flu shot this afternoon.

Name   Date   Helper

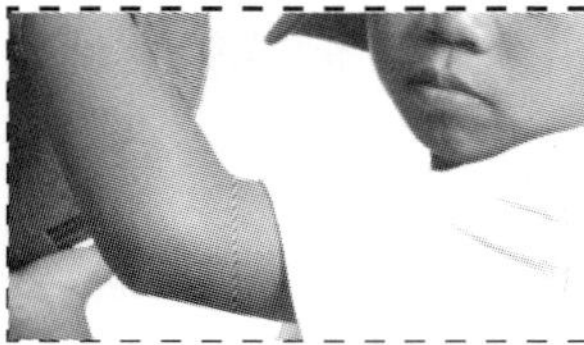 "Let's go practice shooting hoops!"

 "I will help you clean up."

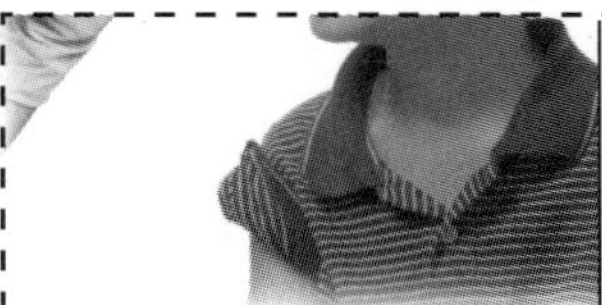 "Flu shots only hurt for a second."

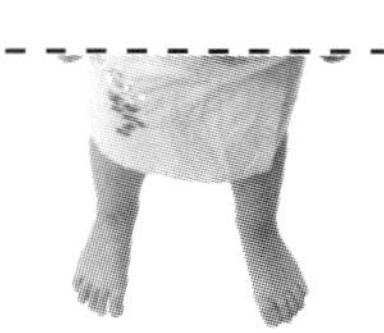 "I will help you clean your dress."

 "Grandpa, can I bring you anything?"

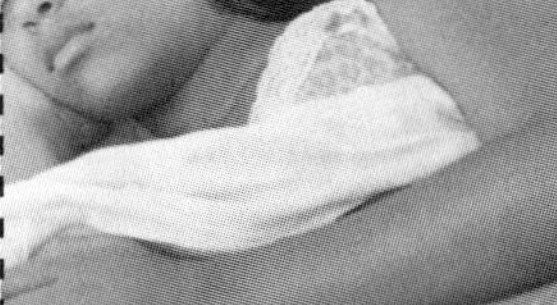 "Let's go visit your friend."

Social Encouragement – Tic-Tac-Toe

Instructions: Cut out the tic-tac-toe markers below. Take turns reading the situations in each box. As you place your marker in a box, tell what you could say or do to make the person feel better. The first player to get three in a row (tic-tac-toe) wins.

Your brother has a black eye and does not want to go to school. 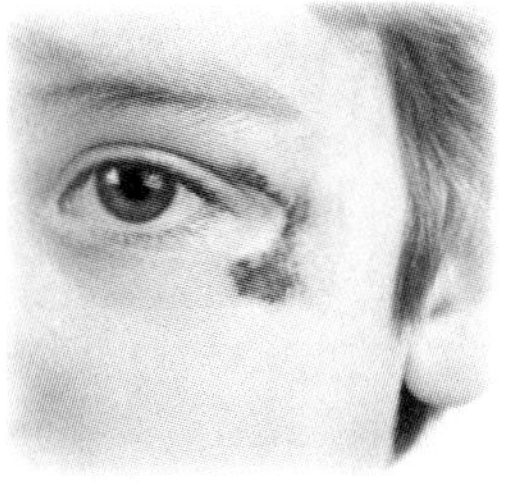	During a sleepover, Sue spills grape juice on your mom's white couch, and she begins to cry. 	Your friend got braces, and she does not like the way she looks. 
Jack's dog is lost, and he has not been able to find him. 	You see a younger student in the hallway who is lost and scared. 	Bobby is feeling sad because he did not make the baseball team. 
Dad is worried about paying bills. 	The football players are discouraged because their team lost every game. 	Mom is annoyed because there are piles of dirty dishes in the sink. 

_______________ _______________ _______________
Name   Date   Helper

X X X X X X

O O O O O O

Social Encouragement – Role-Play

Instructions: Cut out the cards and place them facedown. Player One chooses a card and reads it aloud. Player Two says or does something to help Player One with the problem. Players switch roles in the next round.

Katie is sad because her parents are separating.

Wes misses an easy basket, and his team loses the game.

Nancy is upset because she failed another test.

Aunt Sally's dog died.

Brianna's mom is making her wear her hair in curls for her school picture, and she is embarrassed.

Kathy must start speech therapy, and she does not want to go.

Your friend has a red rash on her face, and she does not want anyone to notice.

Your neighbor is missing her son who is away at college.

Your friend feels hurt because she did not get an invitation to your classmate's party.

______________________   ______________   ________________
Name   Date   Helper

Social Encouragement – Crossword

Instructions: Read the situations below and find the missing words in the Word Bank. Write your answers in the puzzle. Tell what you can say or do to help each person.

Word Bank

team	notice	separating	therapy	tower
college	homework	invitation	recital	braces

Across

2. Your baby brother is crying because his __________ of blocks keeps falling over.

4. Your friend has a red rash on her face, and she does not want anyone to __________.

7. Amanda does the wrong steps in the dance __________ and is embarrassed.

9. Katie is sad because her parents are __________.

10. Your neighbor is missing her son who is away at __________.

Down

1. Michael is frustrated because he doesn't understand his __________.

3. Your friend feels hurt because she did not get an __________ to your classmate's party.

5. Bobby is feeling sad because he did not make the baseball __________.

6. Your friend got __________, and she does not like the way she looks.

8. Kathy must start speech __________, and she does not want to go.

__________________   __________________   __________________

Name   Date   Helper

Social Encouragement – Unscramble

Instructions: Look at each photo and read the situation that goes with it. Then unscramble each sentence to find out what you could say to make the person feel better.

1. Michael is frustrated because he doesn't understand his homework.

You could say:

can	We	our	do	together	homework

"____."

2. Your baby brother is crying because his tower of blocks keeps falling over.

You could say:

help	a	I'll	you	tower	build

"____."

3. You see a younger student in the hallway who is lost and scared.

You could say:

take	your	classroom	I'll	you	to

"____."

4. Jack's dog is lost, and he has not been able to find him.

You could say:

make	Let's	lost	signs	dog	some

"____."

5. Mom is annoyed because there are piles of dirty dishes in the sink.

You could say:

load	dishwasher	I'll	the	you	for

"____."

_______________________________ ____________ _______________________________
Name　　　　　　　　　　　　　　　Date　　　　　　　　　　　Helper

Social Encouragement – Draw a Picture

Instructions: Read each situation and draw a picture in the box that shows what you could do to make the person feel better.

1.

You can tell your teacher is not having a good day.

4.

Bobby is feeling sad because he did not make the baseball team.

2.

Nancy is upset because she failed another test.

5.

Mom is upset because she has too much work to do.

3.

Your sister is worried about her friend who is sick.

6.

Grandma is feeling lonely because she lives by herself.

Name	Date	Helper

Social Encouragement – Five Word Association

Instructions: Write three words that are associated with each photo.

A.

1. _______________________
2. _______________________
3. _______________________

B.

1. _______________________
2. _______________________
3. _______________________

C.

1. _______________________
2. _______________________
3. _______________________

D.

1. _______________________
2. _______________________
3. _______________________

E.

1. _______________________
2. _______________________
3. _______________________

F.

1. _______________________
2. _______________________
3. _______________________

G.
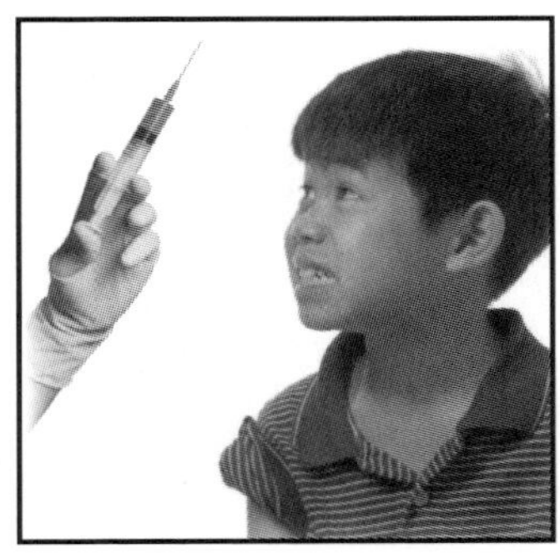

1. _______________________
2. _______________________
3. _______________________

H.
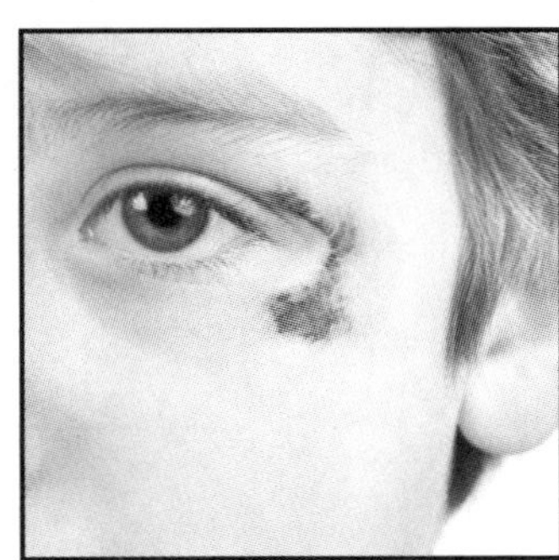

1. _______________________
2. _______________________
3. _______________________

I.

1. _______________________
2. _______________________
3. _______________________

______________________   ______________________   ______________________
Name   Date   Helper

Social Encouragement – Fill It In

Instructions: Look at the photos. Then fill in the blanks with words from the Word Bank to complete the sentences. Tell what you could say or do to make each person feel better.

─────────────────────────── **Word Bank** ───────────────────────────

dress	feelings	ruined	hallway	picture	sleepover
team	couch	curls	list	upset	find
student	lost			basket	failed

1.  Jack's dog is

________________________,

and he has not been able to

________________________ him.

5.  Nancy is

________________________,

because she

____

another test.

2.  Sarah sat on a cupcake and

____

her new

________________________.

6.  Wes misses an easy

________________________,

and his ________________________
loses the game.

3.  You see a younger

____

in the ________________________
who is lost and scared.

7.  Brianna's mom is making
her wear her hair in

____

for her school ________________________
and she is embarrassed.

4.  Charlie's name is not on the

____

for the all-star basketball team,

and his ________________________
are hurt.

8. 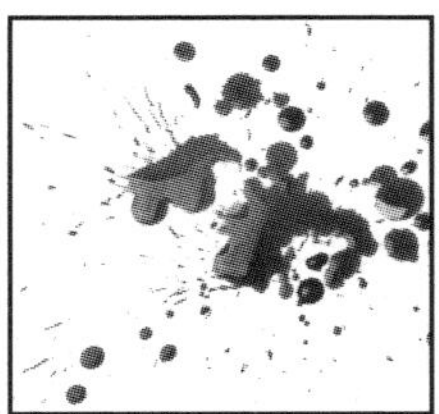 During a

________________________,

Sue spills grape juice on your
mom's white

________________________,

and she begins to cry.

________________________   ________________________   ________________________
Name   Date   Helper

Social Encouragement – Answering Why Questions

Instructions: Look at the photos and read the situations. Then use your imagination to answer the *Why* questions.

1. The football players are discouraged because their team lost every game.
Why have they lost every game?

____

____

____

2. Mom is annoyed because there are piles of dirty dishes in the sink.
Why are there piles of dirty dishes in the sink?

____

____

____

3. Kathy must start speech therapy, and she does not want to go.
Why doesn't Kathy want to go to speech therapy?

____

____

____

4. Mary is angry because her parents will not let her go to the dance.
Why won't Mary's parents let her go to the dance?

____

____

____

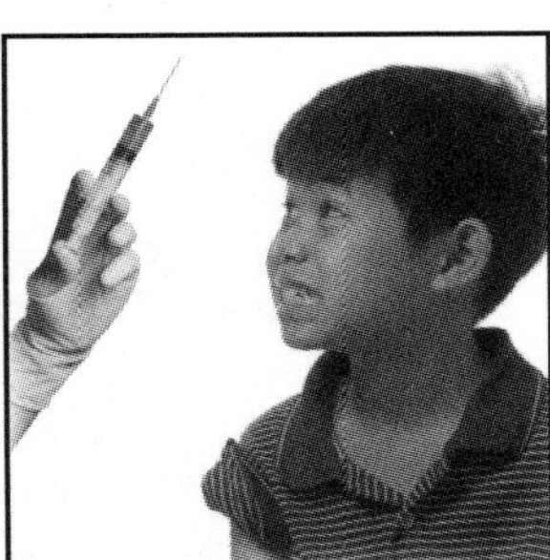

5. Wayne is worried about getting a flu shot this afternoon.
Why is Wayne worried about getting a flu shot?

____

____

____

_____________________ _____________________ _____________________
Name   Date   Helper

Social Encouragement – Ask a Question

Instructions: Look at the photos and read the situations. Write a question that you could ask each person. Then tell what you could say or do to make each person feel better.

1. Aunt Sally's dog died.

2. You see a younger student in the hallway who is lost and scared.

3. Kathy must start speech therapy, and she does not want to go.

4. Your neighbor is missing her son who is away at college.

5. Your friend has a red rash on her face, and she does not want anyone to notice.

Name   Date   Helper

Social Encouragement – Decode the Word

Instructions: Fill in each blank with the correct word. For help, use the Word Bank. Then transfer each letter that has a number under it to reveal the *Secret Word*. Tell what you could say or do to make each person feel better.

Word Bank

worried
frustrated

lonely

sad
discouraged

1.

Michael is

___ ___ ___ ___ ___ ___ ___ ___ ___ ___
(1)
because he doesn't understand his homework.

2.

Dad is

___ ___ ___ ___ ___ ___ ___
   (3)   (4)
about paying bills.

3.

Grandma is feeling

___ ___ ___ ___ ___ ___
         (2)
because she lives by herself.

4.

Katie is ___ ___ ___
            (7)
because her parents are separating.

5.

The football players are

___ ___ ___ ___ ___ ___ ___ ___ ___ ___ ___
(6)(5)
because their team lost every game.

What state is this?

1 2 3 4 5 6 7
Secret Word

___________________ ___________________ ___________________
Name   Date   Helper

Social Encouragement – Nice or Not?

Instructions: Read each situation and the response in quotes. If the response is a nice thing to say, color the *happy* face. If the response is not a nice thing to say, color the *sad* face. For every sad face, give a nice response.

1. Bobby is feeling sad because he did not make the baseball team.

   "I need batting practice too! Let's go to the park!"

2. Wayne is worried about getting a flu shot this afternoon.

   "Oh, no! Flu shots really hurt!"

3. Nancy is upset because she failed another test.

   "Your mom will be so mad! You will probably be punished again!"

4. During a sleepover, Sue spills grape juice on your mom's white couch, and she begins to cry.

   "Don't worry. These things happen."

5. Mom is annoyed because there are piles of dirty dishes in the sink.

   "It's not my fault! It's not my job!"

6. Amanda does the wrong steps in the dance recital and is embarrassed.

   "Really? I didn't even notice! I'm sure no one else noticed, either!"

7. Your friend got braces, and she does not like the way she looks.

   "Almost everyone gets braces. Wait until you see how beautiful your smile will be!"

8. Your friend has a red rash on her face, and she does not want anyone to notice.

   "How did you get that terrible rash?"

___________________________   ___________________   _____________________________
Name   Date   Helper

Social Encouragement – Story Writer

Instructions: Look at the photos and read the situations that go with them. Then write a short story about each one. Think about *who*, *what*, *when*, and *why* for every story.

1.

Jack's dog is lost, and he has not been able to find him.

2.

You can tell your teacher is not having a good day.

3.

Your friend feels hurt because she did not get an invitation to your classmate's party.

Name   Date   Helper

Social Encouragement – What Is It?

Instructions: Look at each photo and read the situation that goes with it. Then write a definition for the word(s) in *italics*. Tell what you could say or do to make each person feel better.

1. Your brother has a *black eye* and does not want to go to school.

   Definition: ____

   ____

2. Katie is sad because her parents are *separating*.

   Definition: ____

   ____

3. Your friend has a red *rash* on her face, and she does not want anyone to notice.

   Definition: ____

   ____

4. Wes *misses* an easy basket, and his team loses the game.

   Definition: ____

   ____

5. Dad is worried about paying *bills*.

   Definition: ____

   ____

| Name | Date | Helper |

Understanding Sarcasm – Match It Up

Instructions: Read each situation below. Under each photo write the number of the situation that matches it. Tell if the person really meant what he/she said.

A. ☐ B. ☐ C. ☐ D. ☐

E. ☐ F. ☐ G. ☐ H. ☐

1. Sara and Raoul are waiting at the bus stop. Sara says, "We're going to be here all day."

2. Clint's favorite team, the Metros, was losing 10 – 0 in the first inning. Clint said, "The Metros are the best team in baseball."

3. Johnny helped Gina get up when she fell on the playground. Gina exclaimed, "Johnny is the sweetest boy in the class."

4. Jeffrey took a bite of cold, soggy french fries and said, "This lunch is delicious!"

5. Jimmy was going on a field trip to the zoo for the 10th time. Jimmy said, "By now, the monkeys know me by my name."

6. Brice yawned and closed his book. He said, "This book is really exciting."

7. Jake and Erin paid $20.00 each to get a ticket, popcorn, and drink for the movie. Jake said, "I'll be 100 before I can save enough money to see another movie."

8. Mom was upset with Dad because he forgot to take the garbage out. Dad said, "I'm sorry honey, I'll do it right now."

Name   Date   Helper

Understanding Sarcasm – Memory Game

Instructions: Cut out the cards. Shuffle and place all cards facedown. Player One chooses two cards to try to match the photo with the corresponding situation. When you make a match, tell whether or not the speaker meant what he/she said. Player Two follows in turn. The player with the most matches wins.

Grandpa tried to leave, but he tripped over his dog lying in front of the door. He said, "Sorry, Gus, I didn't mean to get in your way!"		Gene did math homework for two hours. He was frustrated and said, "I love doing math homework."	
When Mom returned from her morning walk, Dad was still sitting and reading the newspaper. Mom said, "You did a great job cleaning the kitchen while I was gone."		Sally showed up at Laura's costume party wearing her school uniform. Laura said, "Your costume is really scary!"	
Jack's brother Mark burped loudly after his eighth piece of pizza. Jack exclaimed, "You don't like pizza very much, do you?"		Tina and Crystal were walking home in the rain. Their friend John drove by, honked, and waved. Tina said, "John is such a good friend, isn't he?"	
Jennifer asked Jessie what she wanted for her birthday. Jessie said, "I couldn't ask for more than your friendship."		Danny went skiing and had a great time. Danny said, "I can't wait to go skiing again!"	

________________   ________________   ________________
Name   Date   Helper

Understanding Sarcasm – Where Was the Photo Taken?

Instructions: Read each situation and find the photo on the map that matches it. Then write the name of the city where the photo was taken. Tell if the person meant what he/she said.

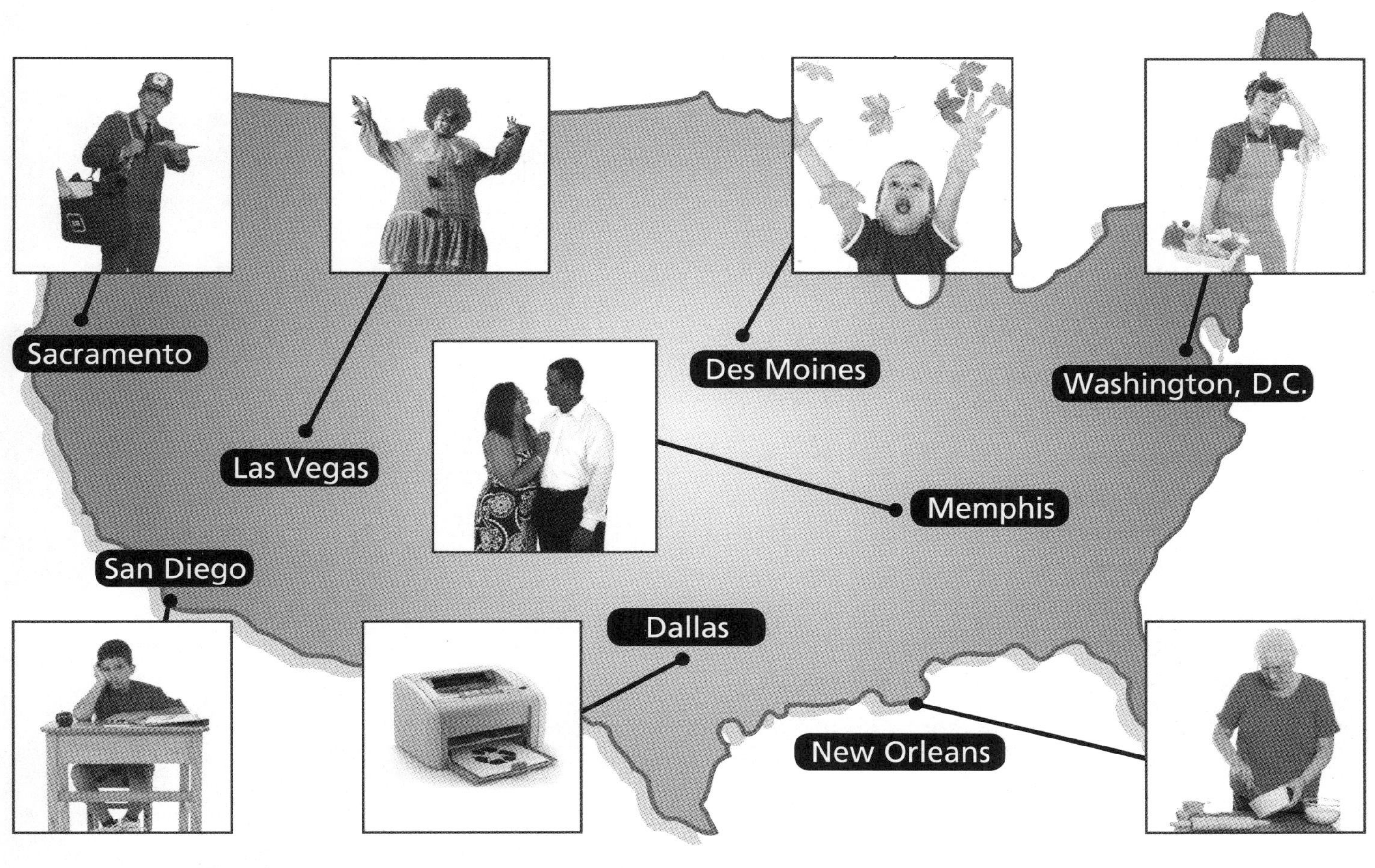

1. Dad looked at Mom when she returned home from the beauty salon. Dad said, "You look like a million dollars!" City – _______________________

2. We laughed at Dad when he put on his costume for Halloween. Dad said, "I'll be the scariest clown in town!" City – _______________________

3. Pete reported for detention again today after school. Pete said to the others, "Detention is my favorite place in the whole world!" City – _______________________

4. We giggled as the leaves were falling faster than we could rake them. Dad said, "I think it is raining leaves!" City – _______________________

5. The computer printer kept printing Chuck's papers with a big, black blob in the center. Chuck said, "This printer works really well." City – _______________________

6. Mom answered the door out of breath, dirty, and sweaty. Mom said to her friend, "Cleaning the house is my favorite pastime." City – _______________________

7. Grandma made Grandpa's favorite food, fried chicken. Grandpa said, "Mmm, I love fried chicken." City – _______________________

8. The mail carrier put the mail in our mailbox, smiled at us, and waved. Dad said, "Our mailman is always so friendly." City – _______________________

_______________________ _______________________ _______________________
Name   Date   Helper

Understanding Sarcasm – Which Response is Sarcastic?

Instructions: Read each situation below. Then circle the response that is sarcastic.

1. Uncle Joe tells a corny joke at the dinner table, but no one laughs. Aunt Sue says,

    A. "That wasn't funny Uncle Joe!"

    B. "That's the funniest joke we've ever heard."

    C. "That joke was terrible."

2. Christy and her brother David were tired and cranky from riding in the car to Grandma's house. David said,

    A. "I hate long car rides."

    B. "That car ride was so boring!"

    C. "When did Grandma move to China?"

3. Jonathan took his smiling little brother to his first grade classroom. Jonathan said to the teacher,

    A. "My brother is just heartbroken about coming to school today!"

    B. "My brother couldn't wait to get here."

    C. "My little brother is a happy camper today!"

4. Laura received an A+ on her math test. Laura said,

    A. "Wow, I did great!"

    B. "That math test was so hard."

    C. "The test was not as hard as I thought."

5. Susie told her sister Becky that she was going to summer school. Becky said,

    A. "Wow, summer school sounds super fun."

    B. "That's too bad. I feel sorry for you."

    C. "Sorry, we'll miss seeing you at the pool."

| Name | Date | Helper |

Understanding Sarcasm – Did They Really Mean That?

Instructions: To assemble the cube, cut on the dotted lines. Fold on the solid lines and glue/tape as indicated. To play, roll the cube. Read the situation on the top side of the cube. Tell if the person meant what he/she said.

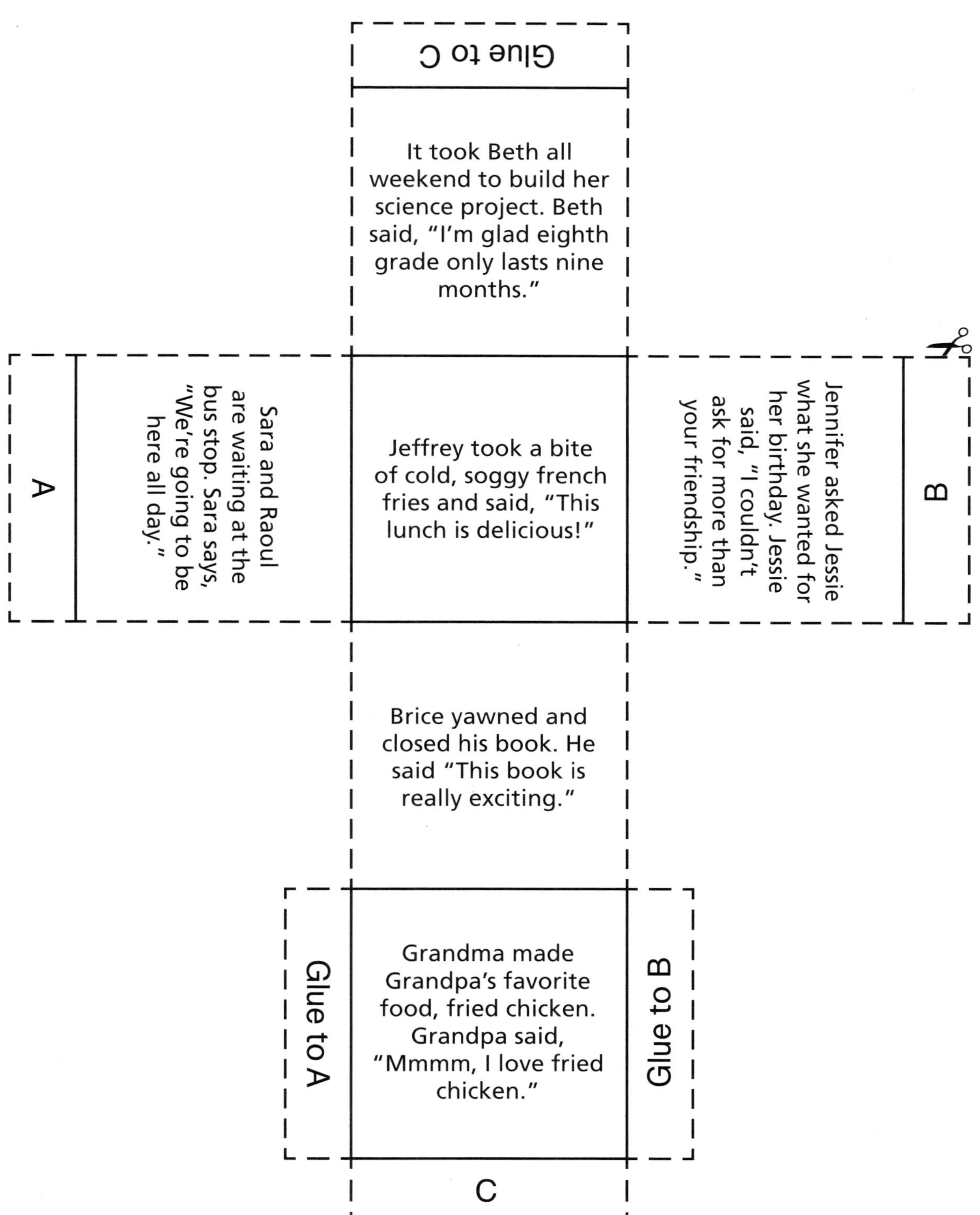

Name	Date	Helper

Understanding Sarcasm – Half-Match

Instructions: Cut out the photos/remarks at the bottom of the page. Then glue/tape them under the matching photos/situations. Tell whether each remark is sincere or sarcastic.

1.  Jeffrey took a bite of cold soggy french fries and said,

4.  The computer printer kept printing Chuck's papers with a big, black blob in the center. Chuck said,

2.  Jack's brother Mark burped loudly after his eighth piece of pizza. Jack exclaimed,

5.  Sally showed up at Laura's costume party wearing her school uniform. Laura said,

3.  Tina and Crystal were walking home in the rain. Their friend John drove by, honked, and waved. Tina said,

6.  We giggled as the leaves were falling faster than we could rake them. Dad said,

---

Name   Date   Helper

 "This printer works really well."

 "This lunch is delicious!"

 "Your costume is really scary!"

 "John is such a good friend, isn't he?"

 "I think it is raining leaves!"

 "You don't like pizza very much, do you?"

Understanding Sarcasm – Game Board

Instructions: To play, cut out game pieces below and place them at "Start." Flip a coin to move. Heads – 1 space. Tails – 2 spaces. As you move around the board, tell if the person meant what he/she said. The first player to reach "Finish" wins.

Clint's favorite team, the Metros, was losing 10–0 in the first inning. Clint said, "The Metros are the best team in baseball."	Johnny helped Gina get up when she fell on the playground. Gina exclaimed, "Johnny is the sweetest boy in the class."	Jimmy was going on a field trip to the zoo for the 10th time. Jimmy said, "By now, the monkeys know me by my name."	Jake and Erin paid $20.00 each to get a ticket, popcorn, and drink for the movie. Jake said, "I'll be 100 before I can save enough money to see another movie."	Mom was upset with Dad because he forgot to take the garbage out. Dad said, "I'm sorry, honey. I'll do it right now."
START				Grandpa tried to leave, but he tripped over his dog lying in front of the door. He said, "Sorry, Gus, I didn't mean to get in your way!"
Tina and Crystal were walking home in the rain. Their friend John drove by, honked, and waved. Tina said, "John is such a good friend, isn't he?"	Jack's brother Mark burped loudly after his eighth piece of pizza. Jack exclaimed, "You don't like pizza very much, do you?"	Sally showed up at Laura's costume party wearing her school uniform. Laura said, "Your costume is really scary!"	Gene did math homework for two hours. He was frustrated and said, "I love doing math homework."	When Mom returned from her morning walk, Dad was still sitting and reading the newspaper. Mom said, "You did a great job cleaning the kitchen while I was gone."
We laughed at Dad when he put on his costume for Halloween. Dad said, "I'll be the scariest clown in town!"				
Danny went skiing and had a great time. Danny said, "I can't wait to go skiing again!"	Dad looked at Mom when she returned home from the beauty salon. Dad said, "You look like a million dollars!"	**FINISH**		

Name   Date   Helper

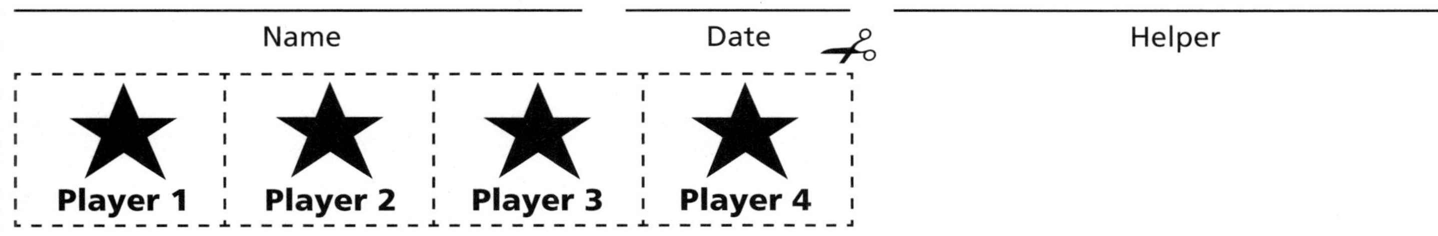

Understanding Sarcasm – Say It Sarcastically or Sincerely

Instructions: Cut out the cards and place them facedown. Player One chooses a card and reads it sarcastically or sincerely. Other players try to guess which way it was said. Once someone guesses, then Player One says the same sentence the opposite way.

Our mailman is always
so friendly.

This printer works
really well.

That's the funniest joke
we've ever heard.

My little brother is a happy
camper today.

I love doing
math homework.

You did a great job
cleaning the kitchen while
I was gone.

Cleaning the house is my
favorite pastime.

Sorry, Gus, I didn't mean to
get in your way.

That math test
was so hard.

______________________   ______________________   ______________________

Name   Date   Helper

Understanding Sarcasm – Tic-Tac-Toe

Instructions: Cut out the tic-tac-toe markers below. Take turns reading the situations in the boxes. Tell if the person means what he/she is saying as you place your marker in a box. The first player to get three in a row (tic-tac-toe) wins.

Pete reported for detention again today after school. Pete said to the others, "Detention is my favorite place in the whole world!" 	We giggled as the leaves were falling faster than we could rake them. Dad said, "I think it is raining leaves!" 	It took Beth all weekend to build her science project. Beth said, "I'm glad eighth grade only lasts nine months." 
Dad looked at Mom when she returned home from the beauty salon. Dad said, "You look like a million dollars!" 	Sara and Raoul are waiting at the bus stop. Sara says, "We're going to be here all day." 	Christy and her brother David were tired and cranky from riding in the car to Grandma's house. David said, "When did Grandma move to China?" 
Tina and Crystal were walking home in the rain. Their friend John drove by, honked, and waved. Tina said, "John is such a good friend, isn't he?" 	Jennifer asked Jessie what she wanted for her birthday. Jessie said, "I couldn't ask for more than your friendship." 	Mom was upset with Dad because he forgot to take the garbage out. Dad said, "I'm sorry, honey. I'll do it right now." 

______________ Name   ______________ Date   ______________ Helper

X X X X X X

O O O O O O

Understanding Sarcasm – Word Search

Instructions: Read each situation below. Find the underlined words in the puzzle. Then tell if each speaker was sincere or sarcastic.

```
S  L  L  K  F  N  O  F  T  N  M  G  E
M  R  O  F  I  N  U  E  P  K  I  Q  X
Y  P  I  Z  Z  A  S  Z  W  H  J  O  C
Q  P  R  K  E  P  F  N  A  D  B  Z  I
R  E  W  I  U  L  Z  B  Y  S  T  J  T
X  R  C  O  G  U  I  Y  G  C  U  S  I
T  K  E  K  R  R  X  M  G  M  M  M  N
C  Y  K  M  T  L  I  J  O  T  L  I  G
K  V  R  H  M  I  D  J  S  D  L  F  J
P  X  D  J  R  U  S  U  I  F  Z  O  O
G  A  Y  R  J  I  S  G  H  H  O  B  Y
Y  M  V  S  Q  Q  W  P  I  U  W  G  I
V  X  Y  F  V  H  Y  X  W  H  V  X  C
```

1. 
Susie told her sister Becky that she was going to <u>summer</u> school. Becky said, "Sorry, we'll miss seeing you at the pool."

2. 
Jeffrey took a bite of cold, <u>soggy</u> french fries and said, "This lunch is delicious!"

3. 
Brice yawned and closed his book. He said, "This book is really <u>exciting</u>."

4. 
Mom was <u>upset</u> with Dad because he forgot to take the garbage out. Dad said, "I'm sorry, honey. I'll do it right now."

5. 
Sally showed up at Laura's costume party wearing her school <u>uniform</u>. Laura said, "Your costume is really scary!"

6. 
Jack's brother Mark burped loudly after his eighth piece of pizza. Jack exclaimed, "You don't like <u>pizza</u> very much, do you?"

7. 
Jennifer asked Jessie what she wanted for her <u>birthday</u>. Jessie said, "I couldn't ask for more than your friendship."

8. 
Pete reported for detention again today after school. Pete said to the others, "Detention is my favorite place in the whole <u>world</u>!"

___________________________   ________________   ________________
Name   Date   Helper

Understanding Sarcasm – Situation-Sarcasm Match

Instructions: Read each situation on the left side of the page. Draw a line from the situation to the appropriate sarcastic remark on the right. Then sarcastically read each remark aloud.

1. 

   Christy and her brother David were tired and cranky from riding in the car to Grandma's house. David said,

   A. "I think it is raining leaves!"

2. 

   Mom answered the door out of breath, dirty, and sweaty. Mom said to her friend,

   B. "When did Grandma move to China?"

3. 

   Uncle Joe tells a corny joke at the dinner table, but no one laughs. Aunt Sue says,

   C. "This printer works really well."

4. 

   The computer printer kept printing Chuck's papers with a big, black blob in the center. Chuck said,

   D. "Cleaning the house is my favorite pastime."

5. 

   We giggled as the leaves were falling faster than we could rake them. Dad said,

   E. "That's the funniest joke we've ever heard."

Name   Date   Helper

Understanding Sarcasm – Say Something Sarcastic

Instructions: Read each situation. Then write your own sarcastic comment about the situation.

1. It took Beth all weekend to build her science project. Beth said,

____

____

____

2. Susie told her sister Becky that she was going to summer school. Becky said,

____

____

____

3. Sara and Raoul are waiting at the bus stop. Sara says,

____

____

____

4. Clint's favorite team, the Metros, was losing 10–0 in the first inning. Clint said,

____

____

____

5. Jimmy was going on a field trip to the zoo for the 10th time. Jimmy said,

____

____

____

6. Jeffrey took a bite of cold, soggy french fries and said,

____

____

____

Name   Date   Helper

Understanding Sarcasm – Fill It In

Instructions: Look at the photos. Then fill in the blanks with words from the Word Bank to complete the sentences. Tell if each person is sincere or sarcastic

---

Word Bank

brother	mailman	skiing	mailbox
cranky	way	tripped	costume
clown	team	love	camper
again	baseball	house	favorite

---

1. Jonathan took his smiling little

   ____

   to his first grade classroom. Jonathan said to the teacher, "My little brother is a happy

   _______________ today!"

2. Grandma made Grandpa's

   _______________ food, fried chicken. Grandpa said,

   "Mmmm, I _______________ fried chicken."

3. The mail carrier put the mail

   in our _______________ , smiled at us, and waved. Dad said,

   "Our _______________ is always so friendly."

4. We laughed at Dad when he

   put on his _______________ for Halloween. Dad said, "I'll

   be the scariest _______________ in town!"

5. Clint's favorite _______________,
   the Metros, was losing 10 – 0 in the first inning. Clint said, "The Metros are the best team in

   _______________ ."

6. Christy and her brother David were tired and

   ____

   from riding the car to Grandma's

   _______________ . David said,
   "When did Grandma move to China?"

7. Grandpa tried to leave, but

   he _______________ over his dog lying in front of the door. He said, "Sorry Gus, I didn't mean to get in your

   _______________ !"

8. Danny went _______________

   and had a great time. Danny said, "I can't wait to go skiing

   _______________ !"

Name _______________   Date _______________   Helper _______________

Understanding Sarcasm – Give a Reason

Instructions: Read each *A* statement in the *Sincere* column in a sincere tone of voice. Read the *B* statement in the *Sarcastic* column in a sarcastic tone of voice. Then write a reason why someone might make each statement.

Sincere	**Sarcastic**

A. My little brother is a happy camper today.

Example: He is going to the movies after school.

B. My little brother is a happy camper today.

Example: He has a lot of homework to do.

A. The Metros are the best team in baseball.

B. The Metros are the best team in baseball.

A. This book is really exciting.

B. This book is really exciting.

A. You did a great job cleaning the kitchen while I was gone.

B. You did a great job cleaning the kitchen while I was gone.

A. I love doing math homework.

B. I love doing math homework.

A. John is such a good friend, isn't he?

B. John is such a good friend, isn't he?

Name   Date   Helper

Understanding Sarcasm – Find the Sarcasm Card

Instructions: Cut out the cards. Shuffle and place them facedown. Player One flips a card, reads the situation, and tells if the remark is sincere or sarcastic. Player Two follows in turn. First player to find the Sarcasm Card wins.

Mom answered the door out of breath, dirty, and sweaty. Mom said to her friend, "Cleaning the house is my favorite pastime."	Uncle Joe tells a corny joke at the dinner table, but no one laughs. Aunt Sue says, "That's the funniest joke we've ever heard."	Danny went skiing and had a great time. Danny said, "I can't wait to go skiing again!"	Jake and Erin paid $20.00 each to get a ticket, popcorn, and drink for the movie. Jake said, "I'll be 100 before I can save enough money to see another movie."
Grandpa tried to leave, but he tripped over his dog lying in front of the door. He said, "Sorry, Gus, I didn't mean to get in your way!"	Johnny helped Gina get up when she fell on the playground. Gina exclaimed, "Johnny is the sweetest boy in the class."	It took Beth all weekend to build her science project. Beth said, "I'm glad eighth grade only lasts nine months."	Mom was upset with Dad because he forgot to take the garbage out. Dad said, "I'm sorry, honey. I'll do it right now."
Sally showed up at Laura's costume party wearing her school uniform. Laura said, "Your costume is really scary!"	Jennifer asked Jessie what she wanted for her birthday. Jessie said, "I couldn't ask for more than your friendship."	Jack's brother Mark burped loudly after his eighth piece of pizza. Jack exclaimed, "You don't like pizza very much, do you?"	We giggled as the leaves were falling faster than we could rake them. Dad said, "I think it is raining leaves!"
Jimmy was going on a field trip to the zoo for the 10th time. Jimmy said, "By now, the monkeys know me by my name."	The computer printer kept printing Chuck's papers with a big, black blob in the center. Chuck said, "This printer works really well."	Grandma made Grandpa's favorite food, fried chicken. Grandpa said, "Mmmm, I love fried chicken."	**Sarcasm** **Card**

___________________   ___________________   ___________________
Name   Date   Helper

Understanding Sarcasm – Decode the Word

Instructions: Fill in each blank with a word to replace the underlined word that tells what the speaker really means. For help, use the Word Bank. Then transfer each letter that has a number under it to reveal the *Secret Word*.

1. Clint's favorite team, the Metros, was losing 10–0 in the first inning. Clint said, "The Metros are the <u>best</u> team in baseball."

——— ——— ——— ——— ——— ———
    ①

Word Bank

easy	boring
hate	worst
	funniest

4. Brice yawned and closed his book. He said, "This book is really <u>exciting</u>."

——— ——— ——— ——— ——— ———
    ④

2. Gene did math homework for two hours. He was frustrated and said, "I <u>love</u> math homework."

——— ——— ——— ———
    ②

5. We laughed at Dad when he put on his costume for Halloween. Dad said, "I'll be the <u>scariest</u> clown in town!"

——— ——— ——— ——— ——— ——— ——— ——— ———
    ③

3. Laura received an *A+* on her math test. Laura said, "That math test was so <u>hard</u>."

——— ——— ——— ——— ———

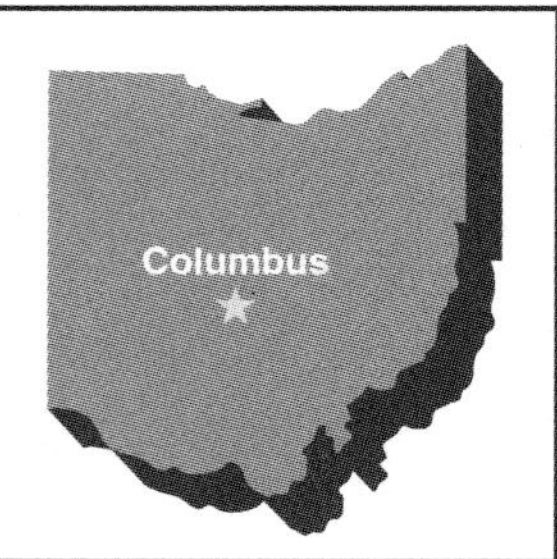

What state is this?

——— ——— ——— ———
 1   2   3   4
Secret Word

_______________________ _______________ _______________________
     Name   Date   Helper

Understanding Sarcasm – Sincere or Sarcastic?

Instructions: Read each situation and remark. If the remark is sincere, color the *happy* face. If the remark is sarcastic, color the *sad* face. For every sad face, give a sincere remark.

1. Johnny helped Gina get up when she fell on the playground. Gina exclaimed, "Johnny is the sweetest boy in the class."

2. Jimmy was going on a field trip to the zoo for the 10th time. Jimmy said, "By now, the monkeys know me by my name."

3. Jeffrey took a bite of cold, soggy french fries and said, "This lunch is delicious!"

4. Danny went skiing and had a great time. Danny said, "I can't wait to go skiing again!"

5. Dad looked at Mom when she returned home from the beauty salon. Dad said, "You look like a million dollars!"

6. We laughed at Dad when he put on his costume for Halloween. Dad said, "I'll be the scariest clown in town!"

7. Pete reported for detention again today after school. Pete said to the others, "Detention is my favorite place in the whole world!"

8. Jack's brother Mark burped loudly after his eighth piece of pizza. Jack exclaimed, "You don't like pizza very much, do you?"

Name	Date	Helper

Understanding Sarcasm – Story Writer

Instructions: Look at the photos and titles below. Write a short story about each one. Try to add a sarcastic remark to each story, and think about *who*, *what*, and *where*.

1. 

At the Bus Stop

2. 

A Terrible Lunch

3.

Horrible Homework

Name   Date   Helper

Understanding Sarcasm – What Is It?

Instructions: Look at each photo and read the situation that goes with it. Then write a defintion for the word in *italics*. Tell if the remark is sincere or sarcastic.

1. Sally showed up at Laura's costume party wearing her school *uniform*. Laura said, "Your costume is really scary!"

   Definition: _______________________________

   ____

   ____

2. The *mail carrier* put the mail in our mailbox, smiled at us, and waved. Dad said, "Our mailman is always so friendly."

   Definition: _______________________________

   ____

   ____

3. Susie told her sister Becky that she was going to *summer* school. Becky said, "Sorry, we'll miss seeing you at the pool."

   Definition: _______________________________

   ____

   ____

4. Clint's favorite team, the Metros, was losing 10–0 in the first inning. Clint said, "The Metros are the best team in *baseball*."

   Definition: _______________________________

   ____

   ____

5. When Mom returned from her morning walk, Dad was still sitting and reading the *newspaper*. Mom said, "You did a great job cleaning the kitchen while I was gone."

   Definition: _______________________________

   ____

   ____

Name	Date	Helper

Understanding Sarcasm – Sincere/Sarcastic Sort

Instructions: Cut out the cards. Pick a card, then read the situation that goes with it. If the remark is sincere, put it in a "sincere" pile. If the remark is sarcastic, put it in a "sarcastic" pile. Then change each sarcastic comment to a sincere comment.

Uncle Joe tells a corny joke at the dinner table, but no one laughs. Aunt Sue says, "That's the funniest joke we've ever heard."

Danny went skiing and had a great time. Danny said, "I can't wait to go skiing again!"

Mom answered the door out of breath, dirty, and sweaty. Mom said to her friend, "Cleaning the house is my favorite pastime."

Jonathan took his smiling little brother to his first grade classroom. Jonathan said to the teacher, "My little brother is a happy camper today!"

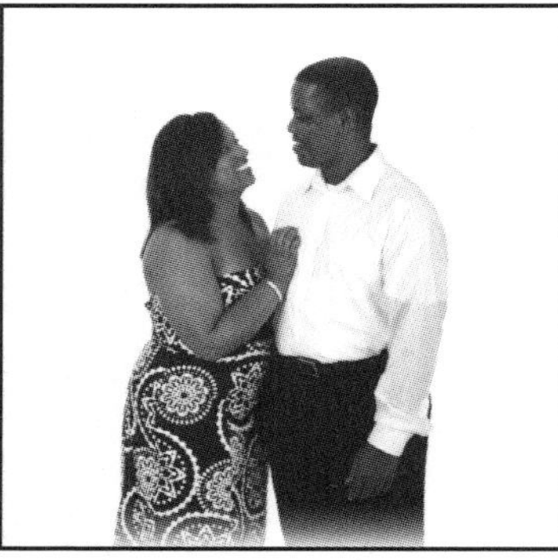

Dad looked at Mom when she returned home from the beauty salon. Dad said, "You look like a million dollars!"

It took Beth all weekend to build her science project. Beth said, "I'm glad eighth grade only lasts nine months."

Christy and her brother David were tired and cranky from riding in the car to Grandma's house. David said, "When did Grandma move to China?"

The mail carrier put the mail in our mailbox, smiled at us, and waved. Dad said, "Our mailman is always so friendly."

Name   Date   Helper

Staying Calm – Match It Up

Instructions: Read each situation below. Under each photo write the number of the situation that matches it. Then tell how you stay calm in each situation.

A.   B.   C.   D.

E.   F.   G.   H.

1. Your teacher assigns five chapters of reading for homework, and you have plans to go to the basketball game tonight.

2. Your younger sibling breaks the piggy bank that your grandparents gave you when you were born. It was your favorite possession!

3. You raise your hand to be the class helper, but the teacher picks your best friend.

4. You come in last place in the championship race after training hard all month.

5. Your barber cut your hair really short after you asked him not to, and you hate it.

6. Your mom talks to you like a baby in front of your friends at the bus stop.

7. The coach asks you to pitch in tonight's game, but she changes her mind and lets a different pitcher play.

8. Your mom puts the wrong sandwich in your lunch bag, and you don't like it.

___________________   ___________________   ___________________
Name   Date   Helper

Staying Calm – Memory Game

Instructions: Cut out the cards. Shuffle and place all cards facedown. Player One chooses two cards to try to match the photo with the corresponding situation. Player Two follows in turn. The player with the most matches wins. When you make a match, tell how to stay calm in that situation.

The hall monitor takes your name to the principal because you are late coming inside for school, but the bell just rang.

You loaned your favorite video game to a friend, and it no longer works.

Your friend asks you to ride the bus to her house. The bus leaves, but your friend doesn't get on.

The teacher asks someone else to deliver a message to the office, and you really want to do it.

Your mom says you cannot get a new skateboard for your birthday because you just got one a few months ago.

Your dad says you cannot have a campout in the backyard, but you already told your friends to come.

Your family is flying to the Bahamas for vacation, but you are afraid to fly.

Your mom says it is time to come inside from playing, but the game you are playing with your friends is tied.

_________________________   _________________________   _________________________
              Name   Date   Helper

Staying Calm – Where Was the Photo Taken?

Instructions: Read each situation and find the photo on the map that matches it. Then write the name of the city where the photo was taken. Tell how to stay calm in each situation.

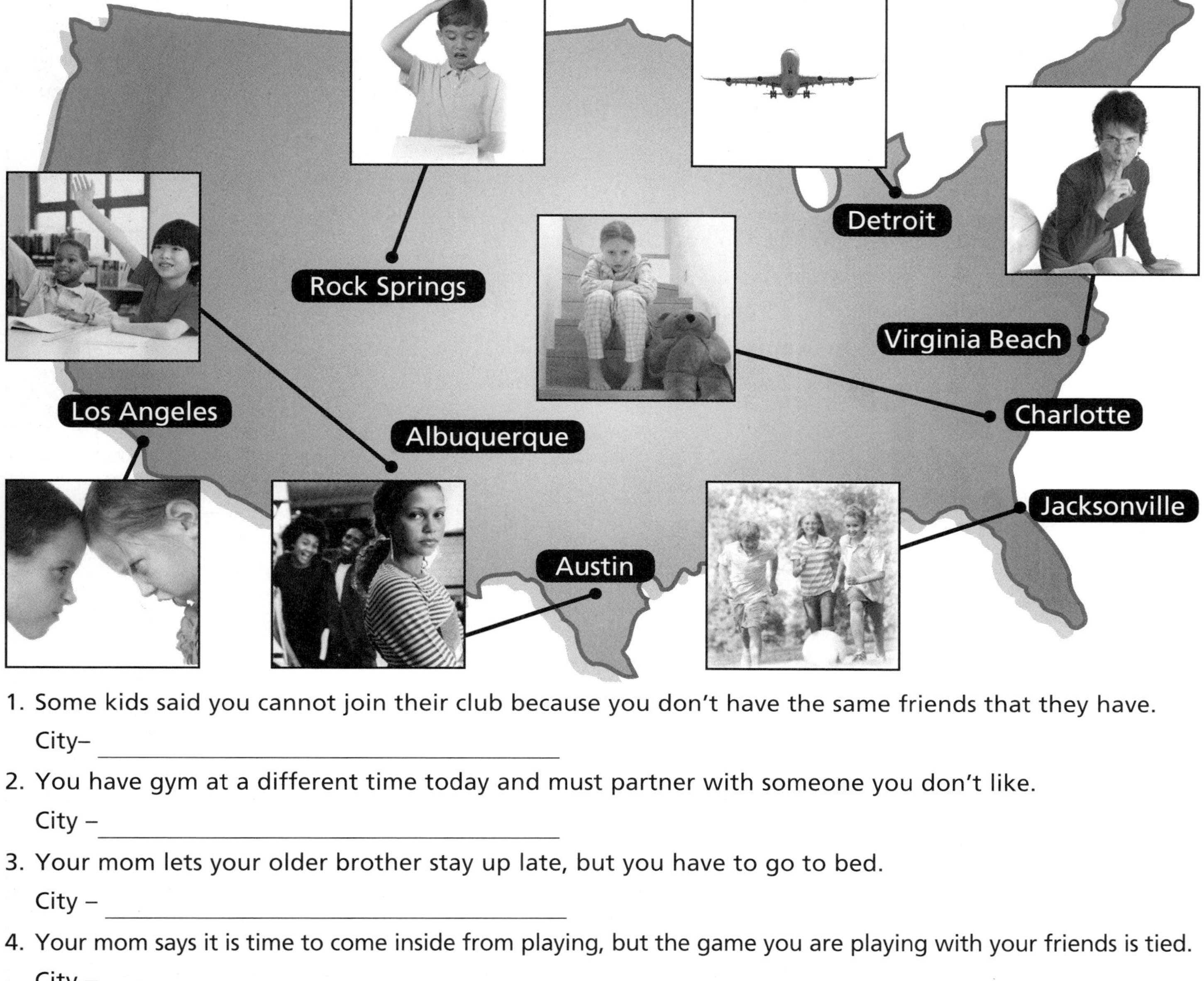

1. Some kids said you cannot join their club because you don't have the same friends that they have.

   City– ___________________________

2. You have gym at a different time today and must partner with someone you don't like.

   City – ___________________________

3. Your mom lets your older brother stay up late, but you have to go to bed.

   City – ___________________________

4. Your mom says it is time to come inside from playing, but the game you are playing with your friends is tied.

   City – ___________________________

5. Your family is flying to the Bahamas for vacation, but you are afraid to fly.

   City – ___________________________

6. You raise your hand to be the class helper, but the teacher picks your best friend.

   City – ___________________________

7. The teacher cancels Fun Friday because a few people in the class are misbehaving, but you aren't.

   City – ___________________________

8. You do not make an *A* on your report, but you think you deserve one because you worked very hard on it.

   City – ___________________________

___________________________ ___________________ ___________________
Name   Date   Helper

Staying Calm – The Best Way

Instructions: Read each situation below. Then circle the best way to stay calm in the situation.

1. Your speech therapy buddy always comes in first in the speech games and gets the best prizes.

   A. Take his prize when he is not looking.

   B. Say you do not want to play anymore.

   C. Be a good sport and tell yourself, "It's just a game."

2. Your mom puts the wrong sandwich in your lunch bag, and you don't like it.

   A. Call your mom and tell her you are angry.

   B. Give it another try and tell yourself, "It's not that bad."

   C. Throw it in the garbage and feel hungry all afternoon.

3. Your teacher says you must rewrite your paper because it is sloppy, but you think it is neat.

   A. Crumple it up and say, "This is not fair!"

   B. Give it another try and tell yourself, "I can always do better."

   C. Tell your teacher that it is neat enough.

4. Your mom talks to you like a baby in front of your friends at the bus stop.

   A. Tell Mom nicely, "Please stop. It is embarrassing."

   B. Yell at Mom and say, "I am not a baby!"

   C. Sit on the sidewalk and pout.

5. A boy in the lunchroom says you are ugly, and his friends laugh. No one will sit at the table with you.

   A. Tell him that he and his friends are ugly.

   B. Just eat alone, because you think no one likes you.

   C. Look for a new table to sit at and tell yourself, "There are plenty of nice kids in the cafeteria."

Name   Date   Helper

Staying Calm – Using Self-Talk

Instructions: To assemble the cube, cut on the dotted lines. Fold on the solid lines and glue/tape as indicated. To play, roll the cube. Read the situation on the top side of the cube. Tell how to stay calm in the situation.

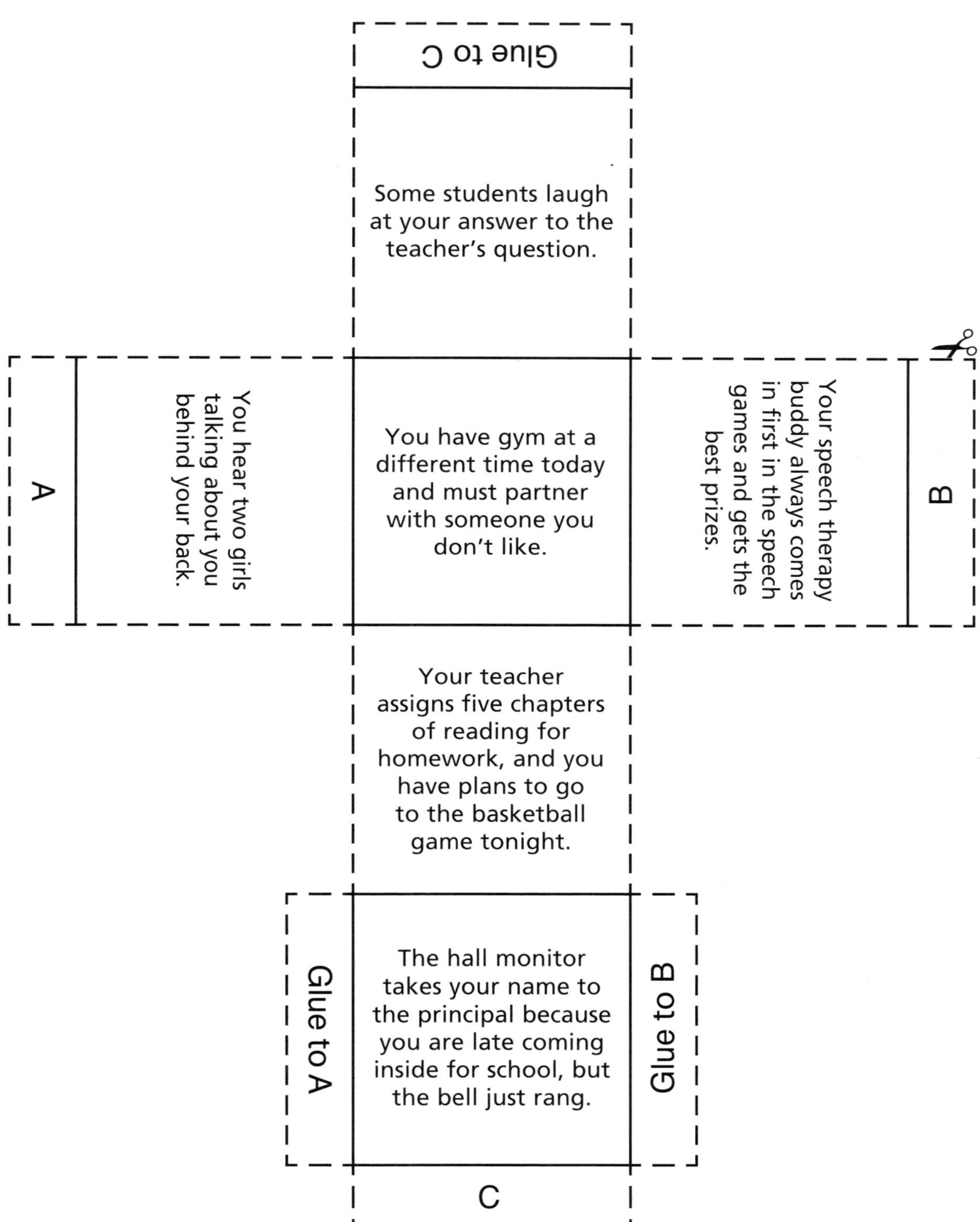

Name   Date   Helper

Staying Calm – Match the Photo

Instructions: Cut out the photos at the bottom of the page. Then glue/tape each photo next to the situation that goes with it. Tell how you stay calm in each situation.

1. Your friend asks you to ride the bus to her house. The bus leaves, but your friend doesn't get on.

4. The coach asks you to pitch in tonight's game, but she changes her mind and lets a different pitcher play.

2. You are the only one not invited to Steve's birthday party tonight, and everyone is laughing at you.

5. Your teacher says that you can't use the computer right now to work on your paper, and you're afraid you'll forget what you want to write.

3. You loaned your favorite video game to a friend, and it no longer works.

6. Your dad says you cannot have a campout in the backyard, but you already told your friends to come.

______________________ ______________________ ______________________
Name   Date   Helper

Staying Calm – Half-Match

Instructions: Cut out the photos/situations at the bottom of the page. Then glue/tape them under the matching photos/situations. Tell how you stay calm in each situation.

1.  A boy in the lunchroom says you are ugly, and his friends laugh.

4.  The hall monitor takes your name to the principal because you are late coming inside for school,

2. You raise your hand to be the class helper,

5.  Your speech therapy buddy always comes in first in the speech games

3. Your mom says you cannot get a new skateboard for your birthday

6.  Some kids said you cannot join their club

---

Name   Date   Helper

 but the bell just rang.

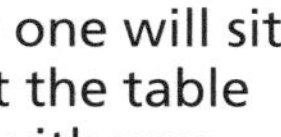 No one will sit at the table with you.

 and gets the best prizes.

 because you just got one a few months ago.

 because you don't have the same friends that they have.

 but the teacher picks your best friend.

Staying Calm – Role-Play

Instructions: Cut out the cards and place them facedown. Player One chooses a card and reads it aloud. Player One explains why the situation may cause a problem. Player Two says something to help Player One stay calm in the situation. Players switch roles in the next round.

Your mom lets your older brother stay up late, but you have to go to bed.

Your dad says you cannot have a campout in the backyard, but you already told your friends to come.

You loaned your favorite video game to a friend, and it no longer works.

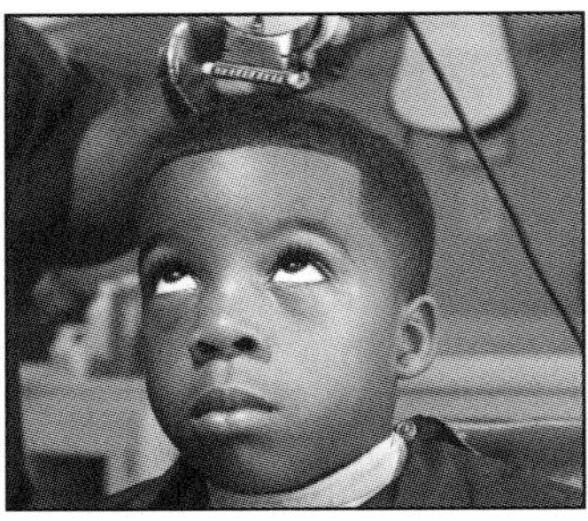

Your barber cut your hair really short after you asked him not to, and you hate it.

Your younger sibling breaks the piggy bank that your grandparents gave you when you were born. It was your favorite possession!

The coach asks you to pitch in tonight's game, but she changes her mind and lets a different pitcher play.

Your mom says you cannot get a new skateboard for your birthday because you just got one a few months ago.

Your teacher says you must rewrite your paper because it is sloppy, but you think is it neat.

The teacher asks someone else to deliver a message to the office, and you really want to do it.

___________________________   _____________   ___________________________
Name   Date   Helper

Staying Calm – Crossword

Instructions: Read the situations below and find the missing words in the Word Bank. Write your answers in the puzzle. Then tell how you would stay calm in each situation.

— Word Bank —

question	birthday	chapters	computer	deserve
tutored	sloppy	monitor	video	group

Across

2. You fail your math test even after being __________ and studying very hard.

5. Someone makes fun of your speech, and then others in the __________ start talking like you and laughing.

8. You do not make an A on your report, but you think you __________ one because you worked very hard on it.

9. Your teacher says you must rewrite your paper because it is __________, but you think it is neat.

10. The hall __________ takes your name to the principal because you are late coming inside for school, but the bell just rang.

Down

1. Your teacher says that you can't use the __________ right now to work on your paper, and you're afraid you'll forget what you want to write.

3. Your teacher assigns five __________ of reading for homework, and you have plans to go to the basketball game tonight.

4. Your mom says you cannot get a new skateboard for your __________ because you just got one a few months ago.

6. Some students laugh at your answer to the teacher's __________.

7. You loaned your favorite __________ game to a friend, and it no longer works.

Name __________   Date __________   Helper __________

Staying Calm – Word Search

Instructions: Read each situation below. Find the words in the puzzle that complete the sentences. For help, use the Word Bank.

Word Bank

flying	lunchroom	misbehaving	training	like
baby	sandwich	report	brother	pitcher

```
D  E  F  Y  L  G  D  R  E  P  C  A  E
W  Y  B  A  B  N  T  K  O  O  T  L  P
M  A  O  R  E  U  I  M  O  C  H  K  O
C  I  N  T  S  L  C  T  R  O  P  E  R
R  B  S  W  I  A  H  O  H  T  B  A  T
E  E  I  B  L  U  N  C  H  R  O  O  M
F  G  H  A  E  R  B  D  T  E  M  R  B
C  L  K  C  L  H  C  B  W  S  R  A  R
H  I  Y  E  T  N  A  F  J  I  H  D  O
I  K  M  I  S  I  H  V  R  M  C  E  T
W  A  C  H  N  R  P  O  I  V  L  H  H
E  I  R  T  H  G  M  A  U  N  M  T  E
S  R  E  T  R  A  I  N  I  N  G  E  R
```

1. You have gym at a different time today and must partner with someone you don't ______.

2. The coach asks you to pitch in tonight's game, but she changes her mind and lets a different __________ play.

3. Your mom lets your older __________ stay up late, but you have to go to bed.

4. Your family is __________ to the Bahamas for vacation, but you are afraid to fly.

5. A boy in the __________ says you are ugly, and his friends laugh. No one will sit at the table with you.

6. You did not make an A on your __________, but you think you deserve one because you worked very hard on it.

7. Your mom talks to you like a __________ in front of your friends at the bus stop.

8. The teacher cancels Fun Friday because a few people in class are __________, but you aren't.

9. Your mom puts the wrong __________ in your lunch bag, and you don't like it.

10. You come in last place in the championship race after __________ hard all month.

Name	Date	Helper

Staying Calm – Unscramble

Instructions: Look at each photo and read the situation that goes with it. Then unscramble the words to tell what you could say to help you stay calm in the situation.

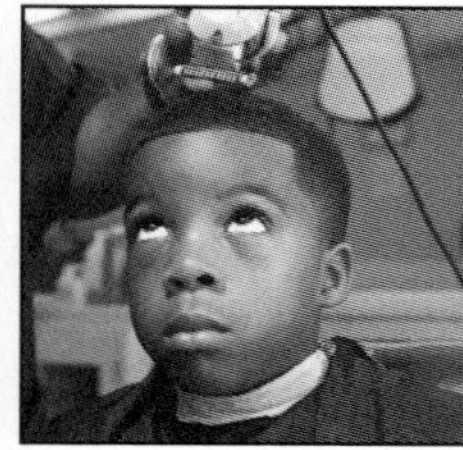

1. Your barber cut your hair really short after you asked him not to, and you hate it. You could say:

hair	Oh	fast	well	my	grows

" ____ ."

2. Your teacher says that you can't use the computer right now to work on your paper, and you're afraid you'll forget what you want to write. You could say:

Staying	will	remember	me	help	focused

" ____ ."

3. Some kids said you cannot join their club because you don't have the same friends that they have. You could say:

can	always	club	my	start	I	own

" ____ ."

4. Some students laugh at your answer to the teacher's question. You could say:

makes	Everyone	mistakes	sometimes

" ____ ."

5. Your younger sibling breaks the piggy bank that your grandparents gave you when you were born. It was your favorite possession! You could say:

know	accident	it	I	was	an

" ____ ."

Name	Date	Helper

Staying Calm – Five Word Association

Instructions: Write five words that are associated with each photo.

A. 

1. _______________________
2. _______________________
3. _______________________
4. _______________________
5. _______________________

B. 

1. _______________________
2. _______________________
3. _______________________
4. _______________________
5. _______________________

C. 

1. _______________________
2. _______________________
3. _______________________
4. _______________________
5. _______________________

D. 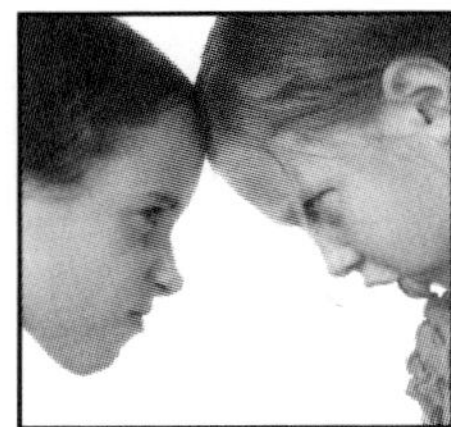

1. _______________________
2. _______________________
3. _______________________
4. _______________________
5. _______________________

E. 

1. _______________________
2. _______________________
3. _______________________
4. _______________________
5. _______________________

F. 

1. _______________________
2. _______________________
3. _______________________
4. _______________________
5. _______________________

G. 

1. _______________________
2. _______________________
3. _______________________
4. _______________________
5. _______________________

H. 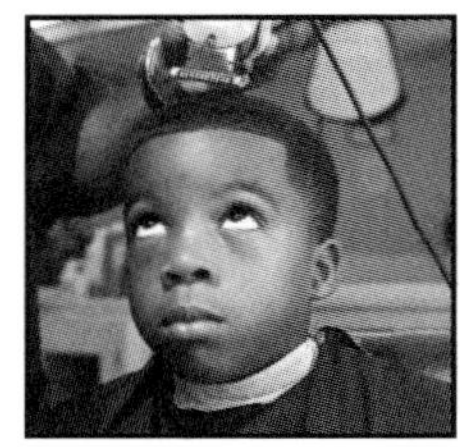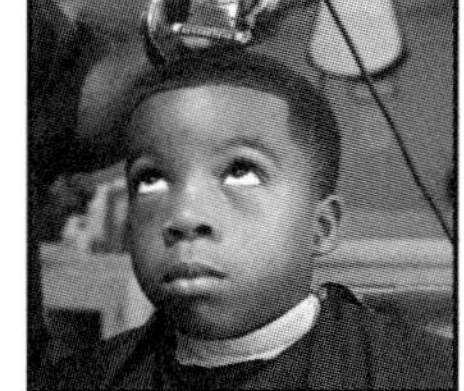

1. _______________________
2. _______________________
3. _______________________
4. _______________________
5. _______________________

I. 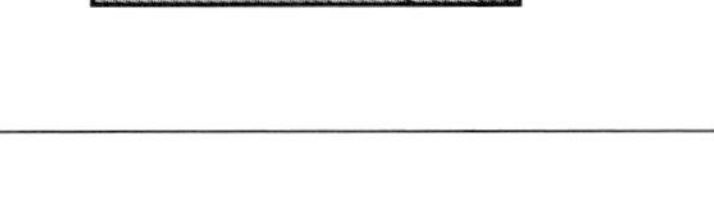

1. _______________________
2. _______________________
3. _______________________
4. _______________________
5. _______________________

___________________ ___________________ ___________________
Name Date Helper

Staying Calm – Fill It In

Instructions: Look at the photos. Then fill in the blanks with words from the Word Bank to complete the sentences. Tell how you stay calm in each situation.

--- **Word Bank** ---

| best | brother | Bahamas | helper | late | lunch | wrong | baby |
| behind | championship | back | afraid | math | studying | training | bus |

1. You raise your hand to be the class ______________ , but the teacher picks your ______________ friend.

5. Your family is flying to the ______________ for vacation, but you are ______________ to fly.

2. Your mom lets your older ______________ stay up ______________ but you have to go to bed.

6. Your mom talks to you like a ______________ in front of your friends at the ______________ stop.

3. Your mom puts the ______________ sandwich in your ______________ bag, and you don't like it.

7. You fail your ______________ test even after being tutored and ______________ very hard.

4. You hear two girls talking about you ______________ your ______________ .

8. You come in last place in the ______________ race after ______________ hard all month.

______________   ______________   ______________

Name   Date   Helper

Staying Calm – Answering Why Questions

Instructions: Look at the photos and read the situations. Then think about each situation from the other person's point of view and answer the *Why* question.

1. Your mom puts the wrong sandwich in your lunch bag, and you don't like it. Why did your mom give you the wrong sandwich?

____

____

2. Your mom says it is time to come inside from playing, but the game you are playing with your friends is tied. Why does your mom want you to come inside?

____

____

3. Your friend asks you to ride the bus to her house. The bus leaves, but your friend doesn't get on. Why doesn't your friend get on the bus?

____

____

4. The coach asks you to pitch in tonight's game, but she changes her mind and lets a different pitcher play. Why does your coach change her mind?

____

____

5. The teacher asks someone else to deliver a message to the office, and you really want to do it. Why does your teacher ask someone else?

____

____

_________________________   _________________   _________________________
Name   Date   Helper

Staying Calm – Ask a Question

Instructions: Look at the photos and read the situations. Write a question you might ask yourself in each situation. Then tell how you stay calm in each situation.

1. You have gym at a different time today and must partner with someone you don't like.

____

____

____

2. Your dad says you cannot have a campout in the backyard, but you already told your friends to come.

____

____

____

3. Your family is flying to the Bahamas for vacation, but you are afraid to fly.

____

____

____

4. You do not make an A on your report, but you think you deserve one because you worked very hard on it.

____

____

____

5. You come in last place in the championship race after training hard all month.

____

____

____

Name   Date   Helper

Staying Calm – Decode the Word

Instructions: Fill in each blank with the correct word. For help, use the Word Bank. Then transfer each letter that has a number under it to reveal the *Secret Word*. Tell how you stay calm in the each situation.

1. Your speech therapy buddy always comes in

___ ___ ___ ___ ___
  ①

in the speech games and gets the best prizes.

Word Bank

class   deliver   stop

first   birthday

4. You are the only one not invited to Steve's

___ ___ ___ ___ ___ ___ ___ ___
           ④

party tonight, and everyone is laughing at you.

2. The teacher asks someone else to

___ ___ ___ ___ ___ ___ ___ a message
 ②

to the office, and you really want to do it.

5. Your mom talks to you like a baby in front

of your friends at the bus ___ ___ ___ ___.
                                          ⑤

3. The teacher cancels Fun Friday because a few people

in the ___ ___ ___ ___ ___ are misbehaving, but
            ③

you aren't.

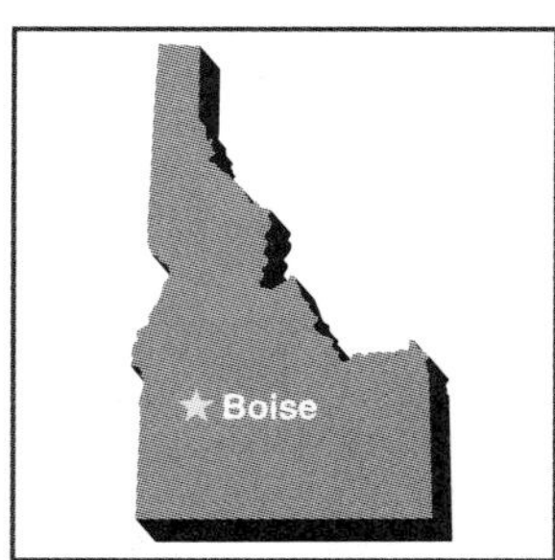

What state is this?

___ ___ ___ ___ ___
 1   2   3   4   5
Secret Word

Name   Date   Helper

Staying Calm – Right or Wrong Self-Talk?

Instructions: Read the situation and the self-talk remark that goes with it. If the remark is something you could tell yourself to stay calm, color the *happy* face. If not, color the *sad* face. For every sad face, change the remark to something you could tell yourself to stay calm.

1. You raise your hand to be the class helper, but the teacher picks your best friend.

   "Maybe she will pick me next time." 

2. The hall monitor takes your name to the principal because you are late coming inside for school, but the bell just rang.

   "Maybe he will listen if I respectfully explain what happened." 

3. The teacher asks someone else to deliver a message to the office, and you really want to do it.

   "This is not fair. She never picks me!" 

4. Someone makes fun of your speech, and then others in the group start talking like you and laughing.

   "I'm never going to speech class again!" 

5. You fail your math test even after being tutored and studying very hard.

   "I'll just keep studying until I do better." 

6. Your mom says it is time to come inside from playing, but the game you are playing with your friends is tied.

   "I'll just ignore her and keep playing." 

7. You have gym at a different time today and must partner with someone you don't like.

   "I'm going to go to the nurse so I can skip gym." 

8. You do not make an A on your report, but you think you deserve one because you worked very hard on it.

   "Next time I will not bother trying so hard." 

Name   Date   Helper

Staying Calm – Story Writer

Instructions: Look at the photos below. Write a short story about each one. Include how to stay calm in each story, and think about *who*, *what*, and *where*.

1.

2.

3.

Name   Date   Helper

Staying Calm – What Is It?

Instructions: Look at each photo and read the situation that goes with it. Then write a definition for the word in *italics*. Tell how to stay calm in each situation.

1. Your teacher says you must rewrite your paper because it is *sloppy*, but you think it is neat.

   Definition: ____

   ____

   ____

2. Your younger sibling breaks the piggy bank that your grandparents gave you when you were born. It was your favorite *possession*!

   Definition: ____

   ____

   ____

3. Your *barber* cut your hair really short after you asked him not to, and you hate it.

   Definition: ____

   ____

   ____

4. You do not make an A on your report, but you think you *deserve* one because you worked very hard on it.

   Definition: ____

   ____

   ____

5. Your speech therapy buddy always comes in first in the speech games and gets the best *prizes.*

   Definition: ____

   ____

   ____

_______________________   _______________________   _______________________
Name   Date   Helper

Staying Calm – What Else Could Have Happened?

Instructions: Read each situation below. Then answer the question about what else could have happened in the situation.

1. The hall monitor takes your name to the principal because you are late coming inside for school, but the bell just rang. *What else could the hall monitor have done?*

____

____

____

2. A boy in the lunchroom says you are ugly, and his friends laugh. No one will sit at the table with you. *What else could the boy's friends have done?*

____

____

____

3. Your dad says you cannot have a campout in the backyard, but you already told your friends to come. *What else could you have done?*

____

____

____

4. You are the only one not invited to Steve's birthday party tonight, and everyone is laughing at you. *What else could everyone have done?*

____

____

____

5. Some students laugh at your answer to the teacher's question. *What else could the students have done?*

____

____

____

___________________________   _______________   ___________________________
Name   Date   Helper

Predicting – Match It Up

Instructions: Read and answer each question below. Under each photo write the number of the question that matches it.

A.   B.   C.   D.

E.   F.   G.   H.

1. What might happen if you leave your bike in the middle of the driveway?

____

2. What might happen if you are sending text messages during class?

____

3. What might happen if you leave the house and forget to put the milk in the refrigerator?

____

4. What might happen if you study very hard for your science test?

____

5. What might happen if your mother catches you sneaking a cookie?

____

6. What might happen if you volunteer at the nursing home?

____

7. What might happen if you break one of your sister's toys?

____

8. What might happen if you forget to do your homework?

____

_________________________ _________________ _________________
Name   Date   Helper

Predicting – Memory Game

Instructions: Cut out the cards. Place all cards facedown. Player One chooses two cards to try to match the question card with the corresponding photo and prediction. Player Two follows in turn. The player with the most matches wins.

What might happen if you practice your trumpet every day?	 You might play the trumpet very well.	What might happen if you are kind and courteous to everyone?	 You might make many people happy.
What might happen if you forget to pack your lunch?	 You might be very hungry.	What might happen if you forget to turn off the water in the bathtub?	 The tub might overflow.
What might happen if you leave the garage door open?	 Someone might steal items from the garage.	What might happen if you leave the door open, and your cat is inside?	 Your cat might run away.
What might happen if you exercise every day and eat healthy foods?	 You might be healthy and strong.	What might happen if you cut in front of someone in the lunch line?	 Someone might be angry.

_______________________ _______________ _______________________
Name   Date   Helper

Predicting – Where Was the Photo Taken?

Instructions: Read and answer each question aloud. Then find the photo on the map that matches it. Write the name of the city where the photo was taken.

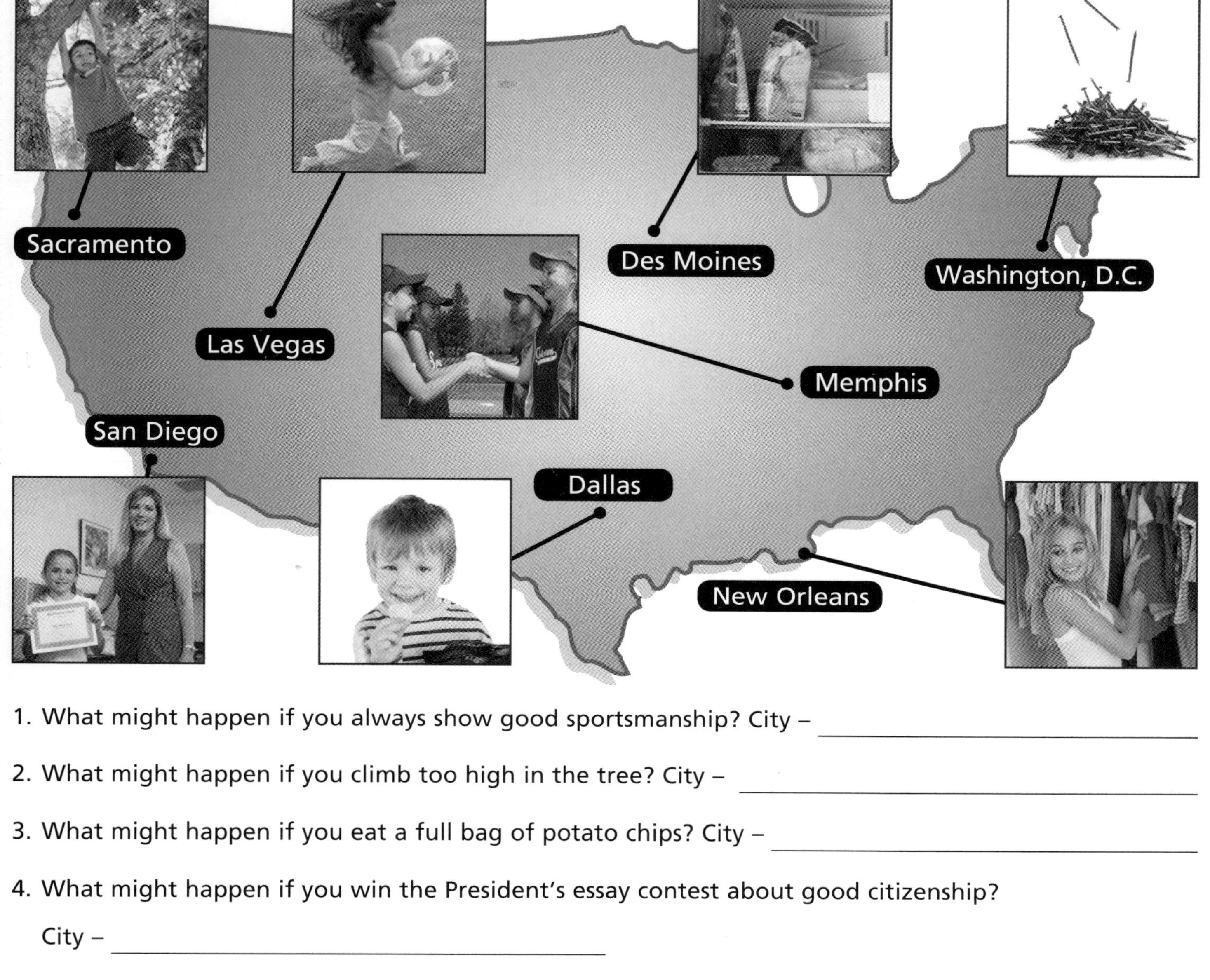

1. What might happen if you always show good sportsmanship? City – ______________________

2. What might happen if you climb too high in the tree? City – ______________________

3. What might happen if you eat a full bag of potato chips? City – ______________________

4. What might happen if you win the President's essay contest about good citizenship?

   City – ______________________

5. What might happen if you wear your sister's favorite dress without her permission?

   City – ______________________

6. What might happen if you don't put on shoes before you go outside to play?

   City – ______________________

7. What might happen if you leave the freezer door open? City – ______________________

8. What might happen if you drop nails in your driveway? City – ______________________

| Name | Date | Helper |

Predicting – The Best Prediction

Instructions: Read each question below. Then circle the best prediction.

1. What might happen if you stay up really late on a school night?

    A. You might get up very early.
    B. You might be very tired in the morning.
    C. You might be very hungry in the morning.

2. What might happen if you are wrestling in the living room and break your mom's favorite vase?

    A. Your mother might be upset.
    B. Your mother might take you to the movies.
    C. Your mother might be proud of you.

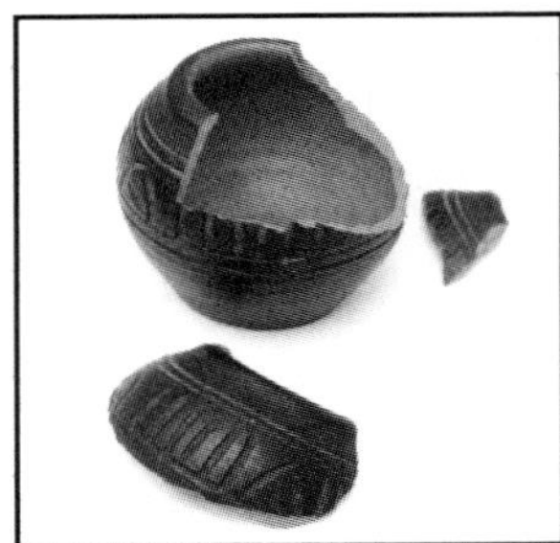

3. What might happen if you shovel the snow from your neighbor's driveway?

    A. Your neighbor might be sad.
    B. Your neighbor might build a snowman.
    C. Your neighbor might be thankful.

4. What might happen if you finish your homework early?

    A. You might go out and play.
    B. You might take out the garbage.
    C. You might do your brother's homework.

5. What might happen if you return a lost wallet?

    A. You might find another wallet.
    B. You might receive a reward.
    C. You might lose your wallet.

Name   Date   Helper

Predicting – What Might Happen If...?

Instructions: To assemble the cube, cut on the dotted lines. Fold on the solid lines and glue/tape as indicated. To play, roll the cube. Read the situation on the top side of the cube. Tell what might happen.

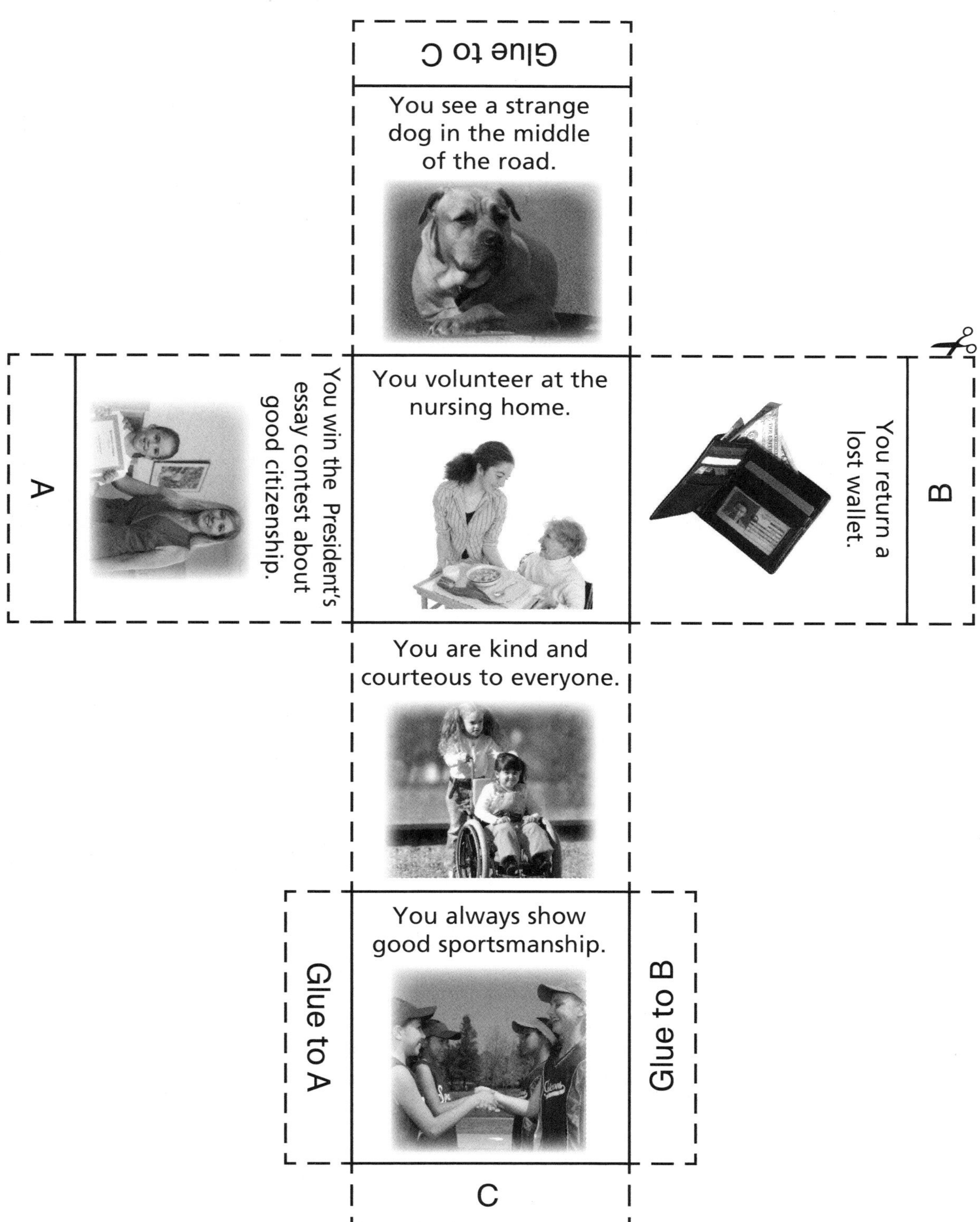

Name   Date   Helper

Predicting – Match the Photo

Instructions: Cut out the photos at the bottom of the page. Then glue/tape each photo next to the prediction that goes with it.

1. You might get in trouble.

4. You might do well on your science test.

2. Your dad might get a flat tire.

5. You might not be able to get down.

3. You might feel sick.

6. The ice cream might melt.

Name   Date   Helper

Predicting – Half-Match

Instructions: Cut out the photos/predictions at the bottom of the page. Then glue/tape them under the matching photos/questions.

1.  What might happen if your mother catches you sneaking a cookie?

2.  What might happen if you leave the house and forget to put the milk in the refrigerator?

3. 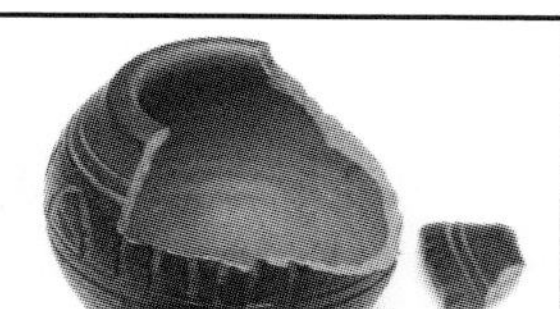 What might happen if you are wrestling in the living room and break your mom's favorite vase?

4.  What might happen if you cut in front of someone in the lunch line?

5.  What might happen if you shovel snow from your neighbor's driveway?

6.  What might happen if you study very hard for your science test?

Name   Date   Helper

 Someone might get angry.

 Your neighbor might be happy.

 You might get an *A*.

 She might be upset.

 You might get punished.

The milk might spoil.

Predicting – How Would You Feel?

Instructions: Read the situations below. Predict how you might feel in each situation and write your answer on the line.

1. You exercise every day and eat healthy foods. You might feel

____

2. You are wrestling in the living room and break your mom's favorite vase. You might feel

____

3. You win the President's essay contest about good citizenship. You might feel

____

4. You volunteer at the nursing home. You might feel

____

5. You see a strange dog in the middle of the road. You might feel

____

Name	Date	Helper

Predicting – Crossword

Instructions: Read the situations below and find the missing words in the Word Bank. Then write your answers in the puzzle.

Word Bank

overflow	tired	feet	upset	outside
trouble	escape	melt	reward	spoil

Across

2. If you are wrestling in the living room and break your mom's favorite vase, she might be __________.

5. If you forget to turn off the water in the bathtub, it might __________.

8. If you leave the house and forget to put the milk in the refrigerator, it might __________.

9. If you stay up really late on a school night, you might be __________.

10. If you return a lost wallet, you might receive a __________.

Down

1. If you leave the door open, and your cat is inside, your cat might __________.

3. If you are sending text messages during class, you might get in __________.

4. If you leave the freezer door open, the ice cream might __________.

6. If you don't put on shoes before you go outside to play, you might hurt your __________.

7. If you finish your homework early, you might play __________.

___________________________ _____________ ___________________________
Name   Date   Helper

Predicting – Word Search

Instructions: Read each situation below. Find the words in the puzzle that complete the sentences. For help, use the Word Bank.

Word Bank

hungry	sick	bike	angry	tire
strong	punished	spoil	detention	down

```
F  N  N  K  C  I  S  N  I  D  E  M  A
Q  O  R  K  O  J  W  Q  E  I  R  T  B
Y  I  N  G  U  O  E  H  S  X  I  E  H
X  T  G  O  D  D  S  T  Q  C  T  W  R
B  N  R  V  Y  I  V  L  H  J  D  A  A
G  E  T  W  N  W  F  S  W  S  N  R  Q
W  T  U  U  M  O  O  Z  T  G  M  Z  C
B  E  P  N  I  A  S  P  R  R  K  K  Y
R  D  H  U  N  G  R  Y  S  Z  O  K  U
V  S  E  V  B  P  X  E  P  R  J  N  Z
T  V  N  K  X  F  W  E  O  Y  I  A  G
S  T  S  N  I  J  P  G  I  D  X  T  L
T  X  N  B  E  B  X  B  L  H  J  A  R
```

1. If you climb too high in the tree, you might not be able to get __________.

2. If you leave your bike in the middle of the driveway, your dad might run over your __________.

3. If your mother catches you sneaking a cookie, you might get __________.

4. If you drop nails in your driveway, Dad might get a flat __________.

5. If you exercise every day and eat healthy foods, you might get __________.

6. If you eat a full bag of potato chips, you might feel __________.

7. If you cut in front of someone in the lunch line, he/she might get __________.

8. If you forget to do your homework, you might get __________.

9. If you forget to pack your lunch, you might be __________.

10. If you leave the house and forget to put the milk in the refrigerator, the milk might __________.

Name	Date	Helper

Predicting – Draw a Picture

Instructions: Read each question and draw a picture in the box that answers the question below it.

1.

What might happen if you exercise every day and eat healthy foods?

2.

What might happen if you stay up really late on a school night?

3.

What might happen if you forget to turn off the water in the bathtub?

4.

What might happen if you don't put on shoes before you go outside to play?

5.

What might happen if you eat a full bag of potato chips?

6.

What might happen if you study very hard for your science test?

Name   Date   Helper

Predicting – Five Word Association

Instructions: Write five words that are associated with each photo.

A.

1. _______________________
2. _______________________
3. _______________________
4. _______________________
5. _______________________

B.

1. _______________________
2. _______________________
3. _______________________
4. _______________________
5. _______________________

C.

1. _______________________
2. _______________________
3. _______________________
4. _______________________
5. _______________________

D.

1. _______________________
2. _______________________
3. _______________________
4. _______________________
5. _______________________

E.

1. _______________________
2. _______________________
3. _______________________
4. _______________________
5. _______________________

F.
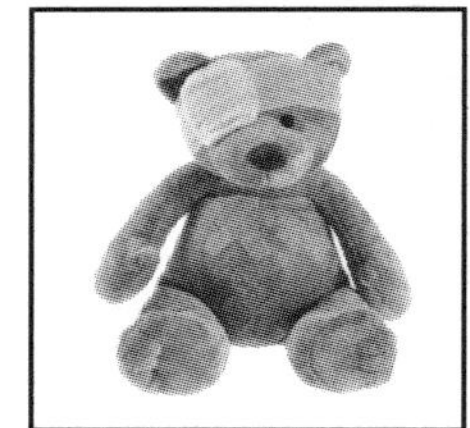

1. _______________________
2. _______________________
3. _______________________
4. _______________________
5. _______________________

G.

1. _______________________
2. _______________________
3. _______________________
4. _______________________
5. _______________________

H.

1. _______________________
2. _______________________
3. _______________________
4. _______________________
5. _______________________

I.

1. _______________________
2. _______________________
3. _______________________
4. _______________________
5. _______________________

_______________________ _______________________ _______________________
Name   Date   Helper

Predicting – Fill It In

Instructions: Look at the photos. Then fill in the blanks with words from the Word Bank to complete the sentences.

Word Bank

freezer	wallet	permission	volunteer	practice	angry	exercise	reward
helpful	citizenship	strong	certificate	sneaking	thaw	punished	improve

---

1.  If you return a lost

   _______________________ ,

   you might receive a

   _______________________ .

5.  If you _______________________

   every day and eat healthy foods,

   you might get _______________________ .

2.  If you leave the

   _______________________ ,

   door open, all the food might

   _______________________ .

6.  If you win the President's essay contest about good

   _______________________ ,

   you might receive a

   _______________________ .

3.  If you _______________________
   your trumpet every day, you

   might _______________________
   your musical skills.

7.  If you wear your sister's favorite dress without her

   _______________________ ,

   she might get

   _______________________ .

4.  If your mother catches you

   _______________________ a cookie,

   you might get _______________________ .

8.  If you _______________________
   at the nursing home, you might

   be very _______________________ .

Name   Date   Helper

Predicting – Answering Why Questions

Instructions: Look at the photos and answer the *Why* questions.

1. Why is it a good idea to exercise every day and eat healthy foods?

____

____

____

2. Why is it a good idea to finish your homework early?

____

____

____

3. Why is it a good idea to study very hard for your science test?

____

____

____

4. Why is it a good idea to practice your trumpet every day?

____

____

____

5. Why is it a good idea to be kind and courteous to everyone?

____

____

____

_______________________________ ______________ _______________________________
Name   Date   Helper

Predicting – Ask a Question

Instructions: Look at each photo and read the answer that goes with it. Then write a question you could ask to get that answer.

1. **Question:** ____

   ____ ?

   Answer: I wrote about good citizenship and won the President's essay contest.

2. **Question:** ____

   ____ ?

   Answer: Johnny left the door open and the cat escaped.

3. **Question:** ____

   ____ ?

   Answer: Joey is stuck in the tree because he climbed too high.

4. **Question:** ____

   ____ ?

   Answer: The ice cream melted because someone left the freezer door open.

5. **Question:** ____

   ____ ?

   Answer: I was sending text messages during class.

Name	Date	Helper

Predicting – Decode the Word

Instructions: Fill in each blank with the correct word. For help, use the Word Bank. Then transfer each letter that has a number under it to reveal the *Secret Word*.

Word Bank

trouble	outside	hungry
angry		reward

1.

If you wear your sister's favorite dress without her permission, she might get

__ __ __ __ __ .
      ⑥

2.

If you forget to pack your lunch, you might get

__ __ __ __ __ __ .
      ④

3.

If you finish your homework early, you might be able to play

__ __ __ __ __ __ __ .
①

4.

If you return a lost wallet, you might receive a

__ __ __ __ __ __ .
      ②

5.

If you are sending text messages during class, you might get in

__ __ __ __ __ __ __ .
    ⑤   ③

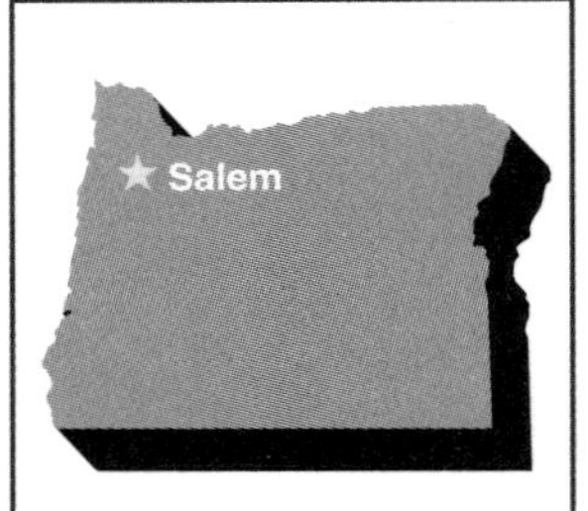

What state is this?

__ __ __ __ __ __
1 2 3 4 5 6
Secret Word

___________________ ___________________ ___________________
     Name   Date   Helper

Predicting – Right or Wrong Prediction?

Instructions: Read each situation. If the prediction makes sense, color the *happy* face. If the prediction does not make sense, color the *sad* face. For every sad face, give a prediction that makes sense.

1. If you forget to do your homework, you might get detention.

2. If you leave the house and forget to put the milk in the refrigerator, you might drink it later.

3. If you are kind and courteous to everyone, you might not have any friends.

4. If you drop nails in your driveway, your dad might get a flat tire.

5. If you break one of your sister's toys, she might give you another toy to play with.

6. If you don't put on shoes before you go outside to play, you might hurt your feet.

7. If you forget to turn off the water in the bathtub, it will overflow.

8. If you leave your bike in the middle of the driveway, your mom might buy you a new bike.

Name	Date	Helper

Predicting – Story Writer

Instructions: Look at the photos and write a short story about each one. Include a prediction about what will happen. Think about *who, what,* and *where* for each story.

1. 

____

____

____

____

____

2.

____

____

____

____

____

3. 

____

____

____

____

____

_________________________ _________________ _________________
Name   Date   Helper

Predicting – What Is It?

Instructions: Look at each photo. Read and answer the question that goes with it. Then write a definition for the word in *italics*.

1. What might happen if you always show good *sportsmanship*?

   Definition: ____

   ____

   ____

2. What might happen if you *practice* your trumpet every day?

   Definition: ____

   ____

   ____

3. What might happen if you are kind and *courteous* to everyone?

   Definition: ____

   ____

   ____

4. What might happen if you wear your sister's favorite dress without her *permission*?

   Definition: ____

   ____

   ____

5. What might happen if your mother catches you *sneaking* a cookie?

   Definition: ____

   ____

   ____

_______________________   _______________________   _______________________
Name   Date   Helper

Predicting – What Else Might Happen?

Instructions: Look at each photo and read the situation. Then write what else might happen in the situation.

1. If you forget to pack your lunch, you might be hungry. *What else might happen?*

____

____

2. If you leave your bike in the middle of the driveway, your dad might run over it. *What else might happen?*

____

____

3. If you stay up really late on a school night, you might be very tired in the morning. *What else might happen?*

____

____

4. If you finish your homework early, you might be able to go outside to play. *What else might happen?*

____

____

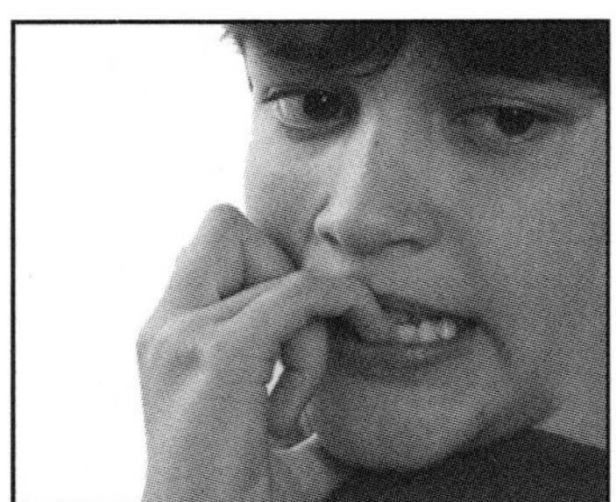

5. If you forget to do your homework, you might get detention. *What else might happen?*

____

____

____ __________________________ ____________________________

| Name | Date | Helper |

Cognitive Flexibility – Match It Up

Instructions: Read each question below. Under each photo write the number that matches the question. Then give two possible answers for each question.

A.

B.

C.

D.

E.

F.

G.

H.

1. Why is your baby brother crying?

____

2. Why is your neighbor's window broken?

____

3. Why is your dad laughing?

____

4. Why are police cars and fire trucks speeding by?

____

5. Why can't Jerry play with his friends?

____

6. Why is Danny late for school?

____

7. Why is Whitney not answering her phone?

____

8. Why is your computer not working?

____

| Name | Date | Helper |

Cognitive Flexibility – Memory Game

Instructions: Cut out the cards. Shuffle and place all cards facedown. Player One chooses two cards to try to match the photo card with the corresponding question. Player Two follows in turn. The player with the most matches wins. When you make a match, give two answers for each question.

Why is Emily lighting a candle?		Why was your sandwich on the table, and now it's gone?	
Why is Sam walking with crutches?		Why is your mom telling you to wear nice clothes?	
Why is Jimmy dirty?		Why is Mary looking at her watch and saying, "Oh no!"	
Why is Tom not at school this morning?		Why is your mom calling your grandma?	

_______________________   _______________   _______________
Name   Date   Helper

Cognitive Flexibility – Where Was the Photo Taken?

Instructions: Read each question aloud and give two answers. Then find the photo on the map that matches the question. Write the name of the city where the photo was taken.

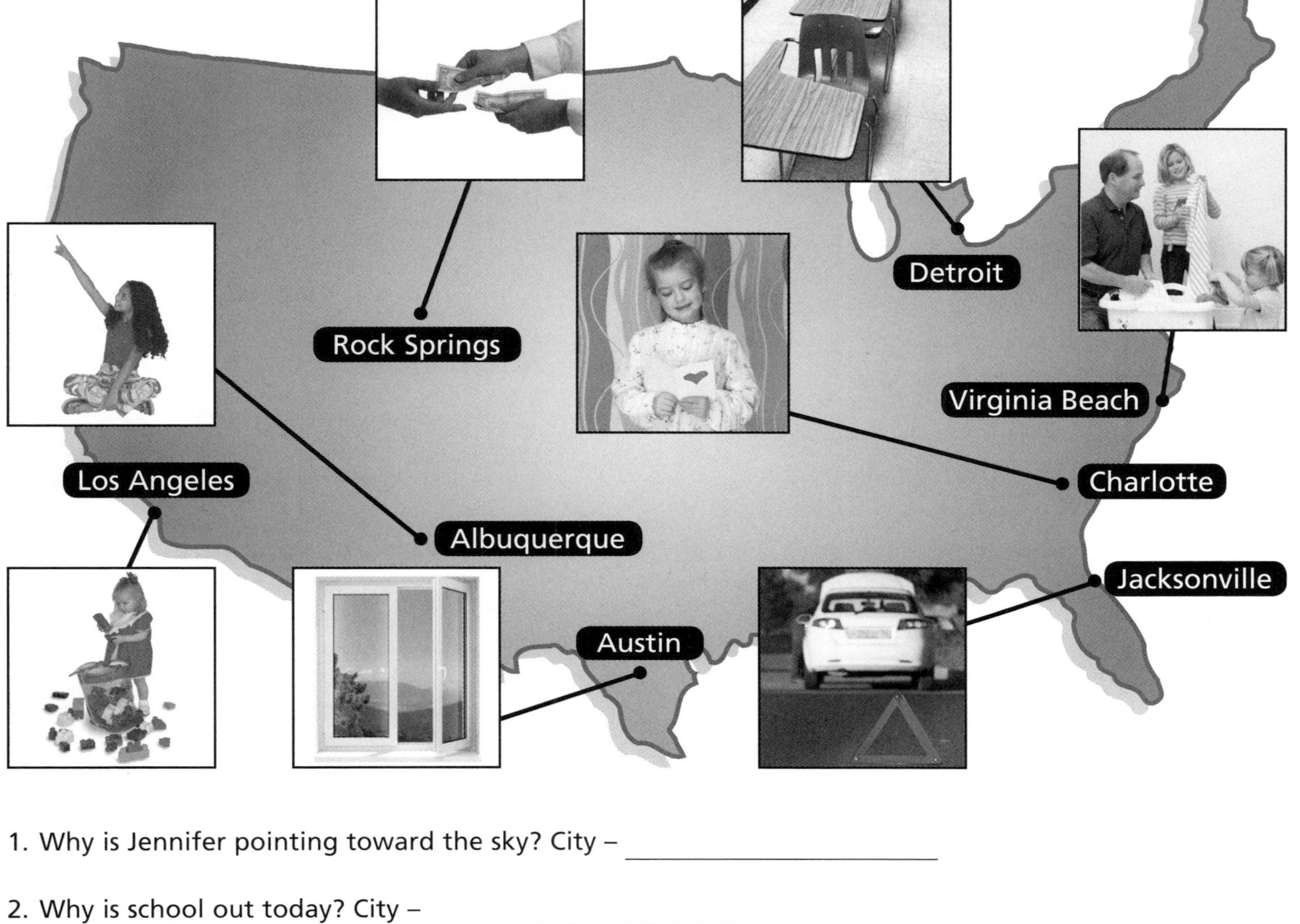

1. Why is Jennifer pointing toward the sky? City – _______________________

2. Why is school out today? City – _______________________

3. Why are your old toys missing? City – _______________________

4. Why did you spend $5.00 today? City – _______________________

5. Why does your dad say he needs you to help more around the house? City – _______________________

6. Why is Kelly reading a letter and smiling? City – _______________________

7. Why are all the windows in the house open? City – _______________________

8. Why is the car stopped in the middle of the street? City – _______________________

_______________________   _______________________   _______________________
Name   Date   Helper

Cognitive Flexibility – The Best Reason

Instructions: Read each question below. Then circle the two best answers for each question.

1. Why is there garbage all over your front yard?

   A. The garbage man threw it there.
   B. A raccoon got into the garbage.
   C. A bad storm blew the garbage can over.

2. Why is your sister not going to the dance?

   A. She is sick.
   B. She doesn't have a date.
   C. She doesn't know when it is.

3. Why are your mom and dad packing their suitcases?

   A. They are going to visit relatives.
   B. They are going on a picnic.
   C. They are coming home from vacation.

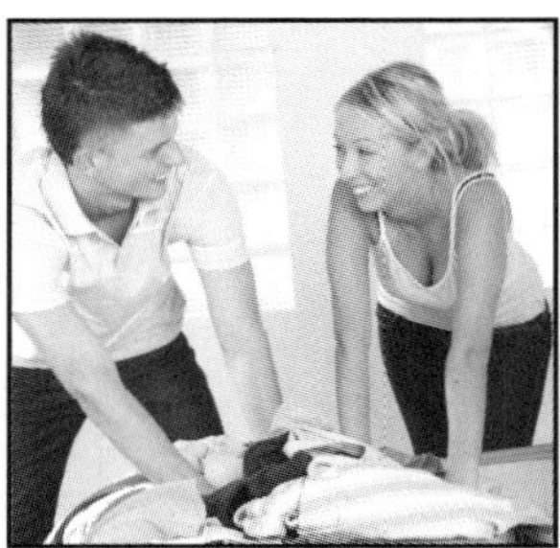

4. Why did your principal say, "May I have your attention, please?"

   A. She wanted to tell you something important.
   B. She wanted to congratulate the winners of the reading contest.
   C. She wanted them to keep talking.

5. Why is the store out of milk?

   A. People heard a hurricane was coming, so they wanted to stock up.
   B. There was a cow shortage.
   C. People bought all of the milk.

Name	Date	Helper

Cognitive Flexibility – Give Two Answers

Instructions: To assemble the cube, cut on the dotted lines. Fold on the solid lines and glue/tape as indicated. To play, roll the cube. Read the question on the top side of the cube. Give two answers for each question.

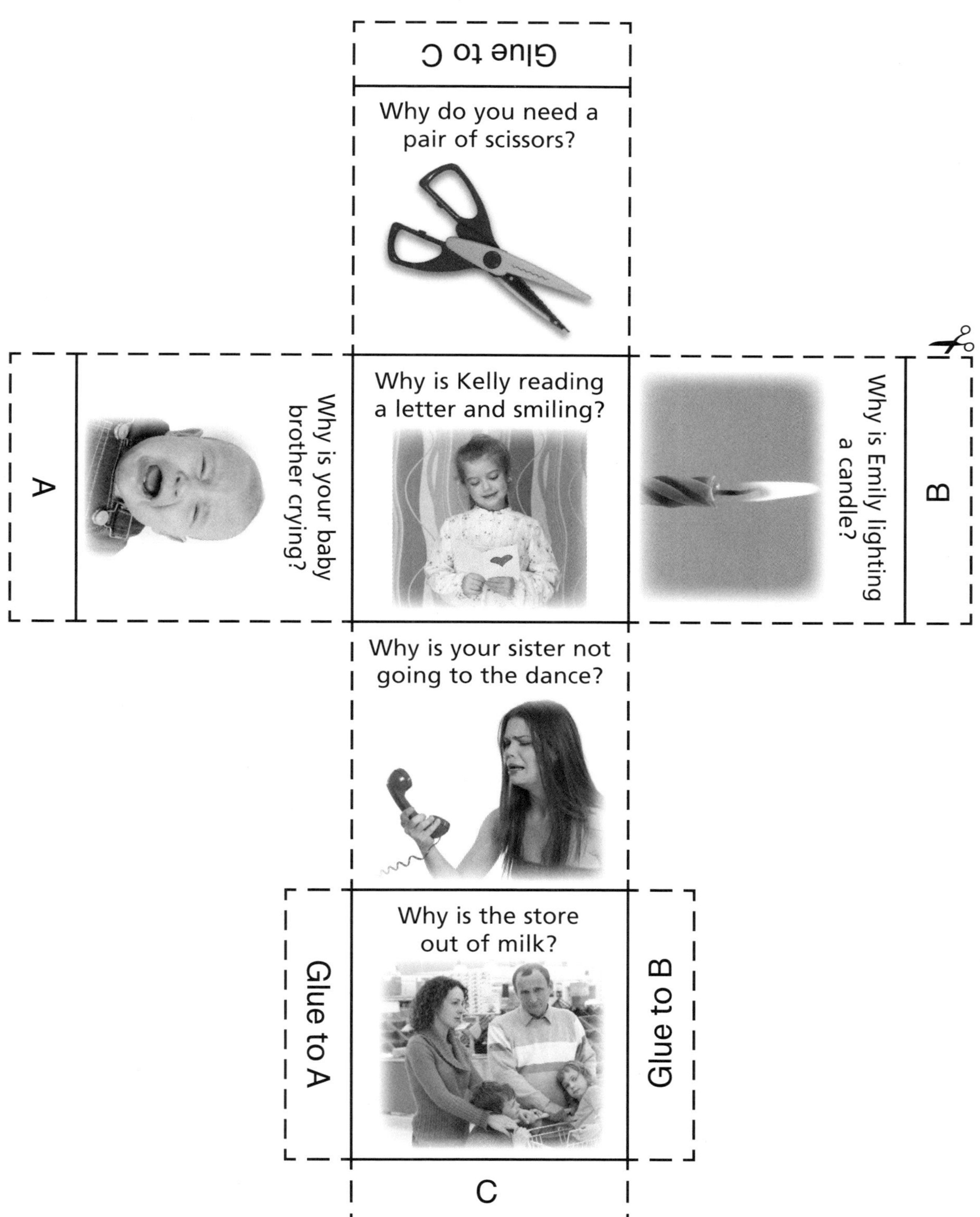

Name   Date   Helper

Cognitive Flexibility – Match the Photo

Instructions: Cut out the photos at the bottom of the page. Then glue/tape each photo next to the question that goes with it. Give two answers for each question.

1.
| Why is your neighbor's window broken? | |

4.
| Why was your sandwich on the table, and now it's gone? | |

2.
| Why did you spend $5.00 today? | |

5.
| Why is Jennifer pointing toward the sky? | |

3.
| Why are all the windows in the house open? | |

6.
| Why do you need a pair of scissors? | |

Name   Date   Helper

#BK-374 *The Question Challenge™ Card Game Fun Sheets* • ©2012 Super Duper® Publications • www.superduperinc.com • 1-800-277-8737

Cognitive Flexibility – Half-Match

Instructions: Cut out the photos/answers at the bottom of the page. Then glue/tape them under the photos/questions they answer.

1. Why is your dad laughing?

4. Why can't Jerry play with his friends?

2. Why is Sam walking with crutches?

5. Why is Mary looking at her watch and saying, "Oh no!"

3. Why is Jimmy dirty?

6. Why is school out today?

_______________ Name _______________ Date _______________ Helper

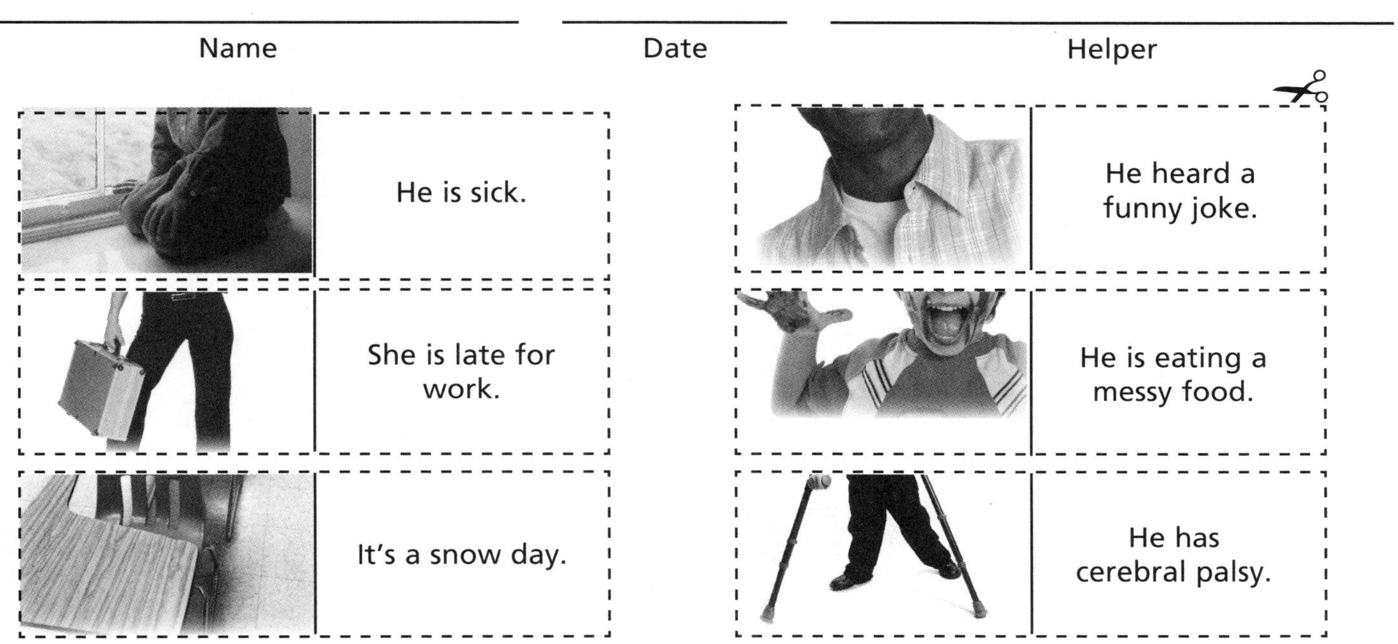

He is sick.

He heard a funny joke.

She is late for work.

He is eating a messy food.

It's a snow day.

He has cerebral palsy.

Cognitive Flexibility – Tic-Tac-Toe

Instructions: Cut out the tic-tac-toe markers below. Take turns reading a question in each box. Give two answers for each question as you place your marker in a box. The first player to get three in a row (tic-tac-toe) wins.

Why is your dad laughing? 	Why is your mom telling you to wear nice clothes? 	Why are your old toys missing? 
Why did your principal say, "May I have your attention, please?" 	Why does your dad say he needs you to help more around the house? 	Why are police cars and fire trucks speeding by? 
Why is your mom calling your grandma? 	Why is school out today? 	Why is the car stopped in the middle of the street? 

_______________________   _______________________   _______________________
Name   Date   Helper

X X X X X X

O O O O O O

Cognitive Flexibility Game Board

Instructions: To play, cut out game pieces below and [place them on] "Start." Flip a coin to move. Heads – 1 space. Tails – 2 spaces. As you move around the [board, give your] opinion for each statement you land on. The first player to reach "Finish" win[s].

Why can't Jerry play with his friends?

Why is Danny late for school?

[Why is] your computer [n]ot working?

Why is Sam walking with crutches?

START

Why is Jimmy dirty?

Why is Mary looking at her watch and saying, "Oh no!"

Why is Tom not at school this morning?

Why is there garbage all over your front yard?

Why are your mom and dad packing their suitcases?

Why is your baby brother crying?

Why is your dad laughing?

Why are police cars and fire trucks speeding by?

Why was your sandwich on the table, and now it's gone?

Why is your mom telling you to wear nice clothes?

Why is your neighbor's window broken?

FINISH

Name	Date	Helper

Player 1

Player 2

Player 3

Player 4

Cognitive Flexibility – Crossword

Instructions: Read each question below and find the word in the Word Bank that means the opposite of the underlined word. Write the word in the puzzle. Give two answers for each question.

Word Bank

dirty	crying	out	late	smiling
friends	spend	old	laughing	open

Across

4. Why is Jimmy <u>clean</u>?

5. Why is your dad <u>crying</u>?

6. Why is your baby brother <u>laughing</u>?

7. Why is school <u>in</u> today?

8. Why did you <u>earn</u> $5.00 today?

Down

1. Why is Kelly reading a letter and <u>frowning</u>?

2. Why are all the windows in the house <u>closed</u>?

3. Why can't Jerry play with his <u>enemies</u>?

5. Why is Danny <u>early</u> for school?

7. Why are your <u>new</u> toys missing?

<u>Name</u>   <u>Date</u>   <u>Helper</u>

Cognitive Flexibility – Word Search

Instructions: Read each question, and find the underlined word in the puzzle. Give two answers for each question.

```
E  G  S  P  L  T  Y  X  N  T  S  W  M
V  L  U  P  W  A  U  M  J  X  C  U  R
H  C  D  L  E  C  J  C  D  X  I  B  C
B  C  H  N  E  N  O  U  B  C  Y  K  S
Z  Z  O  Y  A  M  D  J  R  R  Y  P  L
O  H  M  I  P  C  A  U  N  J  W  M  O
P  Z  M  U  S  E  H  C  T  U  R  C  O
A  W  T  H  W  A  T  C  H  T  P  S  H
X  E  N  O  U  T  Z  S  F  W  Z  H  C
R  E  B  U  K  C  P  R  E  D  P  J  S
D  M  M  S  M  C  M  B  R  N  G  W  J
C  Q  P  E  A  O  A  S  C  F  L  S  O
W  R  P  M  M  Q  V  T  I  N  B  Q  D
```

1. Why is Whitney not answering her <u>phone</u>?

2. Why is your <u>computer</u> not working?

3. Why is Emily lighting a <u>candle</u>?

4. Why is Sam walking with <u>crutches</u>?

5. Why is Mary looking at her <u>watch</u> and saying, "Oh no"?

6. Why is Tom not at <u>school</u> this morning?

7. Why is your <u>mom</u> calling your grandma?

8. Why is Jennifer pointing toward the <u>sky</u>?

9. Why did you <u>spend</u> $5.00 today?

10. Why does your dad say he needs you to help more around the <u>house</u>?

_________________________ _________________________ _________________________
Name   Date   Helper

Cognitive Flexibility – Unscramble

Instructions: Unscramble each question, and rewrite it on the line. Give two answers for each question.

1. 

   Emily   Why   is   lighting   candle   a

   ____ ?

2. 

   Sam   crutches   Why   walking   with   is

   ____ ?

3. 

   school   is   Why   today   out

   ____ ?

4. 

   are   missing   toys   old   Why   your

   ____ ?

5. 

   did   spend   you   Why $5.00   today

   ____ ?

_________________________   ______________   _________________
Name   Date   Helper

Cognitive Flexibility – Fill It In

Instructions: Look at the photos. Then fill in the blanks with words from the Word Bank to complete the questions. Give two answers for each question.

Word Bank

car	dad	please	street	garbage	working	wear	watch
clothes	no	yard	suitcases	computer	table	attention	gone

1. 1. Why is the _______________ stopped in the middle of the _______________?

2. Why is your _______________ not _______________?

3. Why is there _______________ all over your front _______________?

4. Why was your sandwich on the _______________, and now it's _______________?

5. Why are your mom and _______________ packing their _______________?

6. Why is your mom telling you to _______________ nice _______________?

7. Why did your principal say, "May I have your _______________, _______________?"

8. Why is Mary looking at her _______________ and saying, "Oh _______________!"

_______________________   _______________   _______________________
Name   Date   Helper

Cognitive Flexibility – Answering Why Questions

Instructions: Look at the photos, and then answer the *Why* questions with your own predictions.

1. Why is your sister not going to the dance?

____

____

____

2. Why is the store out of milk?

____

____

____

3. Why do you need a pair of scissors?

____

____

____

4. Why is Whitney not answering her phone?

____

____

____

5. Why is your computer not working?

____

____

____

_________________________   _________________   _________________
Name   Date   Helper

Cognitive Flexibility – Ask a Question

Instructions: Look at the photos and answers. Then write a question that goes with each one. Give one more answer for your question aloud.

1. **Question:** ____

   ____ ?

   Answer: You need scissors to cut paper.

2. **Question:** ____

   ____ ?

   Answer: The store is out of milk because the milk shipment didn't arrive.

3. **Question:** ____

   ____ ?

   Answer: I spent $5.00 because I needed to buy lunch.

4. **Question:** ____

   ____ ?

   Answer: School is out today because it is a holiday.

5. **Question:** ____

   ____ ?

   Answer: Jennifer is pointing toward the sky because she sees a shooting star.

________________________   ________________   ________________

Name   Date   Helper

Cognitive Flexibility – Decode the Word

Instructions: Fill in each blank with the correct word. (The word is the "main idea" for the answer.) Then transfer each letter that has a number under it to reveal the *Secret Word*.

Word Bank

| doctor | announcement | vacation | sick | raccoon |

1.

Why did your principal say,
"May I have your attention, please?"

___ ___ ___ ___ ___ ___ ___ ___ ___ ___ ___ ___
  ①   ②

2.

Why is there garbage
all over your front yard?

___ ___ ___ ___ ___ ___ ___
  ④

3.

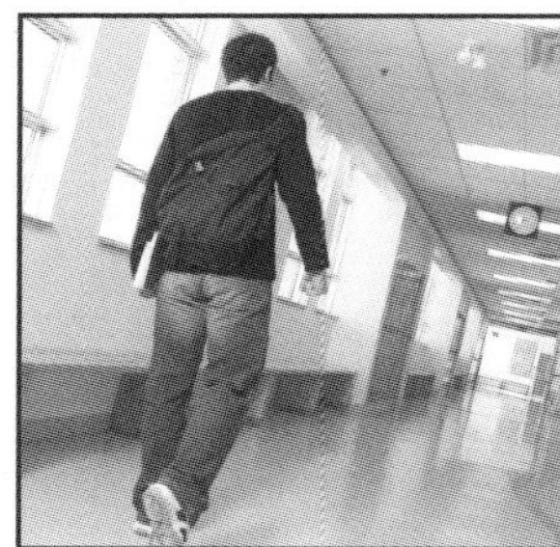

Why is Danny late for school?

___ ___ ___ ___
⑤

4.

Why are your mom and
dad packing their suitcases?

___ ___ ___ ___ ___ ___ ___ ___
③   ⑥

5.

Why is Tom not at
school this morning?

___ ___ ___ ___

What state is this?

___ ___ ___ ___ ___ ___
1 2 3 4 5 6
Secret Word

___________________   ___________   ___________
Name   Date   Helper

Cognitive Flexibility – Right or Wrong Answer?

Instructions: Read each question. If the answer makes sense, color the *happy* face. If the answer does not make sense, color the *sad* face. Give another answer for each happy face you color. For every sad face, give an answer that makes sense.

1. Why is your neighbor's window broken?

   Answer: Someone threw a rock through it.

2. Why are police cars and fire trucks speeding by?

   Answer: There is a fire in the neighborhood.

3. Why can't Jerry play with his friends?

   Answer: He finished all his homework.

4. Why is Jimmy dirty?

   Answer: He was playing with paints.

5. Why is your mom calling your grandma?

   Answer: She is inviting her to dinner.

6. Why does your dad say he needs you to help more around the house?

   Answer: Mom is very lazy.

7. Why is Kelly reading a letter and smiling?

   Answer: She got some bad news.

8. Why are all the windows in the house open?

   Answer: It's a nice day, and they want some fresh air.

| Name | Date | Helper |

Cognitive Flexibility – Write Three Reasons

Instructions: Look at the photos and questions. Then write three answers for each question.

1. Why are all the windows open in the house?

   Answer 1: ____

   Answer 2: ____

   Answer 3: ____

2. Why is your baby brother crying?

   Answer 1: ____

   Answer 2: ____

   Answer 3: ____

3. Why is the car stopped in the middle of the street?

   Answer 1: ____

   Answer 2: ____

   Answer 3: ____

_______________________   _______________________   _______________________
          Name   Date   Helper

Cognitive Flexibility – What Is It?

Instructions: Look at each photo and the question that goes with it. Then write a definition for the word in *italics*. Give an answer for each question aloud.

1. Why is Emily lighting a *candle*?

   Definition: ____

   ____

   ____

2. Why was your sandwich on the *table*, and now it's gone?

   Definition: ____

   ____

   ____

3. Why is Mary looking at her *watch* and saying, "Oh no!"?

   Definition: ____

   ____

   ____

4. Why is the *car* stopped in the middle of the street?

   Definition: ____

   ____

   ____

5. Why did your *principal* say, "May I have your attention, please?"

   Definition: ____

   ____

   ____

Name	Date	Helper

Cognitive Flexibility – Question-Answer Match

Instructions: Look at the photos and read each question on the left side of the page. Draw a line from the question to the best answer on the right side of the page.

1. 
Why is your sister not going to the dance?

   A. You are going to a nice restaurant.

2. 
Why are your old toys missing?

   B. The electricity went off.

3. 
Why is your mom telling you to wear nice clothes?

   C. She is not allowed to use her phone in school.

4. 
Why is Emily lighting a candle?

   D. Mom donated them to a charity.

5. 
Why is Whitney not answering her phone?

   E. Her boyfriend broke up with her.

Name   Date   Helper

Questioning in Conversation – Match It Up

Instructions: Read each statement below. Under each photo write the number of the statement that matches it. Then write a question you could ask about each statement.

A.   B.   C.   D.

E.   F.   G.   H.

1. There is going to be an assembly in school tomorrow.

____

2. I am moving away.

____

3. We're going out to celebrate tonight.

____

4. I saw a great movie last night.

____

5. I went shopping for new clothes last weekend.

____

6. There was an accident in my neighborhood.

____

7. I'm joining a new after-school program.

____

8. I have a new cell phone.

____

___________________________________ ___________________ ___________________
Name   Date   Helper

Questioning in Conversation – Memory Game

Instructions: Cut out the cards. Shuffle and place all cards facedown. Player One chooses two cards to try to match the photo with the corresponding statement. Player Two follows in turn. The player with the most matches wins. When you make a match, ask three questions about the statement.

My sister won the biggest trophy.

My teacher was upset with the class today.

I bought a new video game.

I read some great books this summer.

I finished my Halloween costume.

I broke my arm.

My dog ran away.

LOST DOG

My family is going on vacation.

______________________________ ______________ ______________________________
Name   Date   Helper

Questioning in Conversation – Where Was the Photo Taken?

Instructions: Read each statement and find the photo on the map that matches it. Then write the name of the city where the photo was taken. Choose any four statements, and ask three questions about each one.

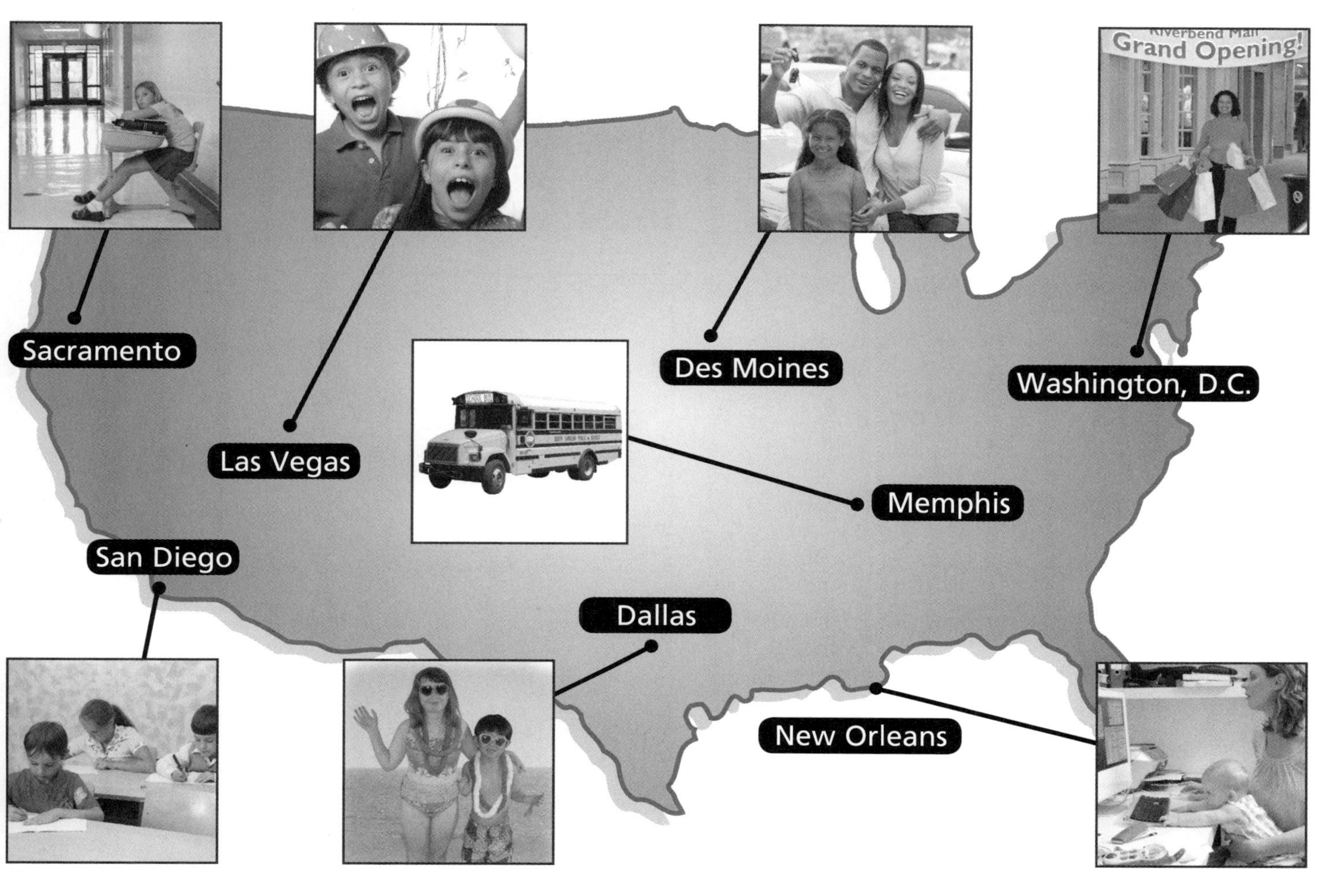

1. I didn't go to school yesterday. City– _______________________

2. I have detention. City – _______________________

3. Our family just bought a new car. City – _______________________

4. There's a new mall opening in town today. City – _______________________

5. There is going to be a surprise party for Mary. City – _______________________

6. Let's go to the beach. City – _______________________

7. My mom ordered tickets online for the concert. City – _______________________

8. Today, the school bus broke down. City – _______________________

___________________________ ___________________ ___________________________
Name   Date   Helper

Questioning in Conversation – The Best Question

Instructions: Read each statement. Then circle the question that most directly relates to the statement.

1. They are closing the park early.

    A. Where is the park?
    B. Why is the park closing early?
    C. Did you see the new swings at the park?

2. The teacher needs some helpers after class.

    A. Who helped her the last time?
    B. Where is the teacher?
    C. What does she need help with?

3. I'm going to visit my grandmother.

    A. Where does she live?
    B. How old is she?
    C. Is she nice?

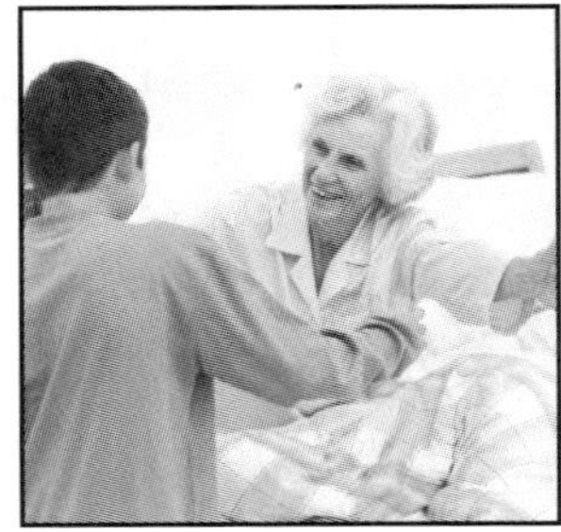

4. I finished my science project.

    A. Do you like your science teacher?
    B. What did you do your project on?
    C. Is science your favorite class?

5. I saw a police officer in front of the bank.

    A. Was there a bank robbery?
    B. Did she say hello to you?
    C. Was she mad?

Name	Date	Helper

Questioning in Conversation – Ask Three Questions

Instructions: To assemble the cube, cut on the dotted lines. Fold on the solid lines and glue/tape as indicated. To play, roll the cube. Read the statement on the top side of the cube. Ask three questions about the statement.

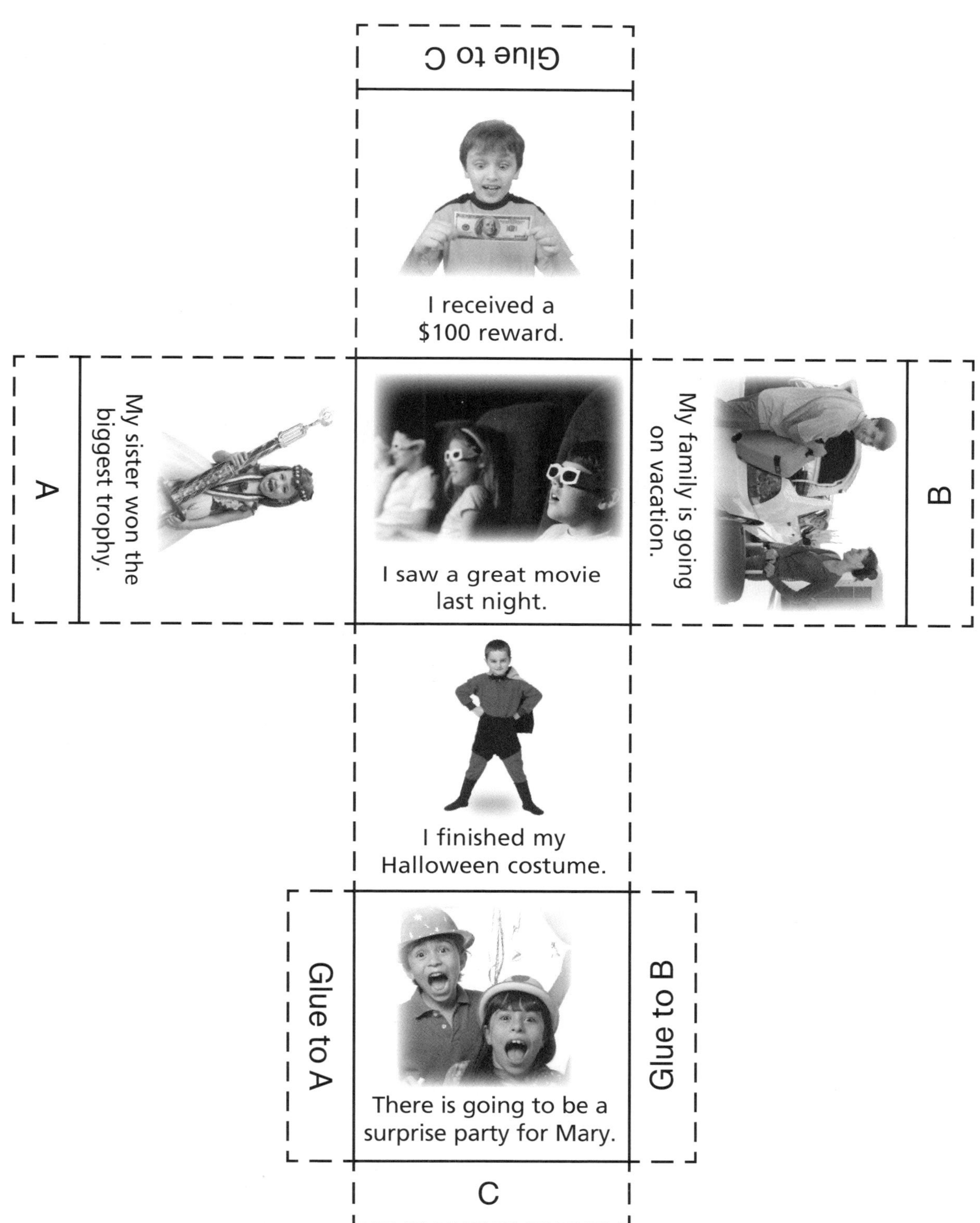

___________________ ___________________ ___________________
Name   Date   Helper

Questioning in Conversation – Match the Photo

Instructions: Cut out the photos at the bottom of the page. Then glue/tape each photo next to the statement that goes with it. Ask three questions about each statement.

1. There is going to be an assembly in school tomorrow.

4. We're going out to celebrate tonight.

2. I went shopping for new clothes last weekend.

5. My teacher was upset with the class today.

3. I broke my arm.

6. They are closing the park early.

Name   Date   Helper

  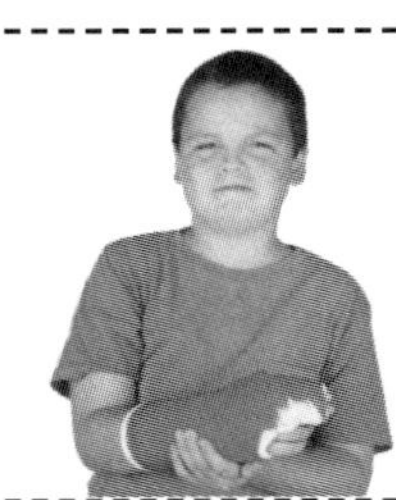   

Questioning in Conversation – Half-Match

Instructions: Cut out the photos/questions at the bottom of the page. Then glue/tape them under the matching photos/statements.

1. I have a new cell phone.

2. My sister won the biggest trophy.

3. I finished my science project.

4. I am moving away.

5. I'm going to visit my grandmother.

6. I saw a great movie last night.

______________________ ______________________ ______________________
Name   Date   Helper

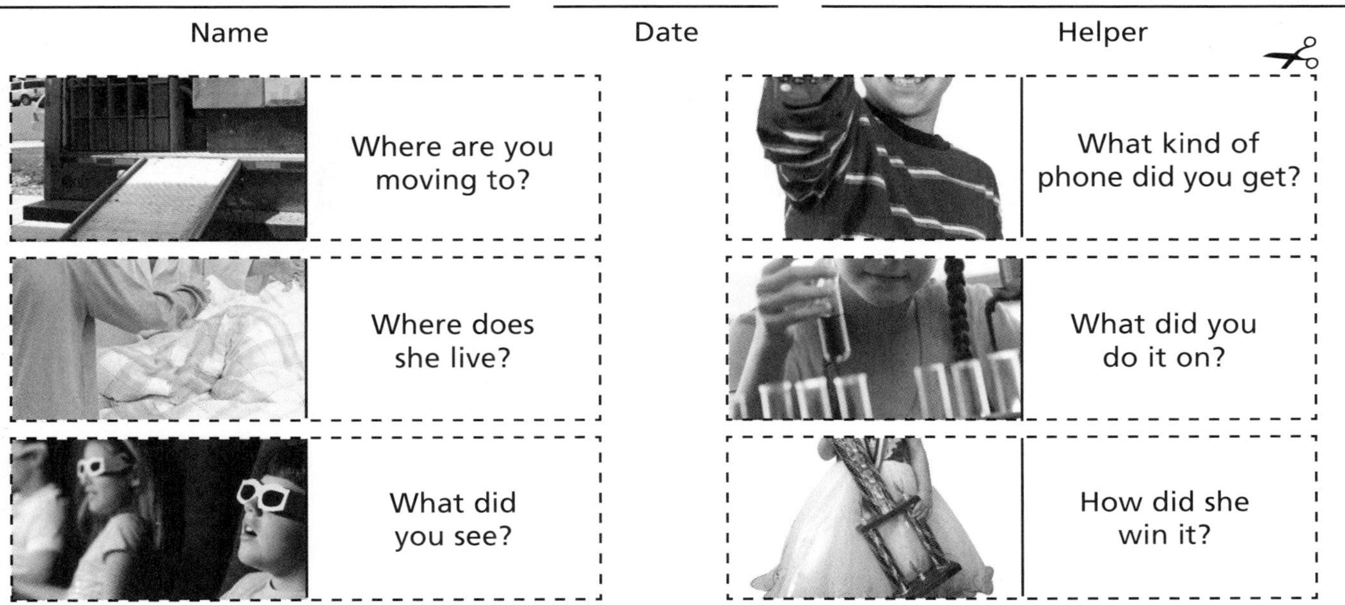

Questioning in Conversation – Game Board

Instructions: To play, cut out game pieces below and place them at "Start." Flip a coin to move. Heads – 1 space. Tails – 2 spaces. As you move around the board, ask three questions about each statement. The first player to reach "Finish" wins.

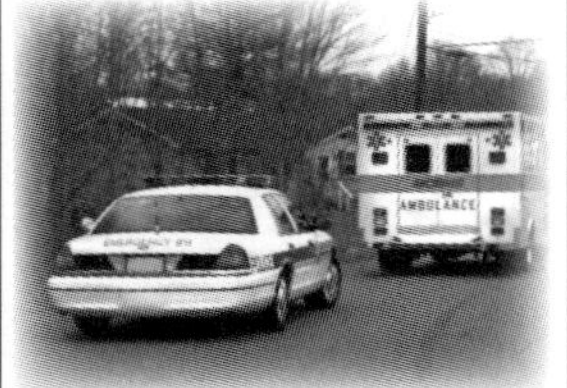

There was an accident in my neighborhood.

I have a new cell phone.

I am moving away.

I'm joining a new after-school program.

I bought a new video game.

START

I read some great books this summer.

Our family just bought a new car.

I have detention.

I didn't go to school yesterday.

My family is going on vacation.

My dog ran away.

There's a new mall opening in town today.

FINISH

Let's go to the beach.

My mom ordered tickets online for the concert.

Today, the school bus broke down.

The teacher needs some helpers after class.

I'm going to visit my grandmother.

_______________________ ______________
Name   Date   Helper

★ **Player 1** ★ **Player 2** ★ **Player 3** ★ **Player 4**

Questioning in Conversation – Tic-Tac-Toe

Instructions: Cut out the tic-tac-toe markers below. Choose a box and read the statement in it. Ask three questions about the statement. Place your marker in the box. The first player to get three in a row (tic-tac-toe) wins.

Name   Date   Helper

Questioning in Conversation – Crossword

Instructions: Read each statement below and find the missing word in the Word Bank. Write the word in the puzzle. Then choose five statements and ask three questions that relate to each one.

Word Bank

assembly	dog	new	books	clothes
program	vacation	party	Halloween	video

Across

3. My __________ ran away.

4. I'm joining a new after-school __________.

8. There is going to be a surprise __________ for Mary.

9. There is going to be an __________ in school tomorrow.

10. I finished my __________ costume.

Down

1. I read some great __________ this summer.

2. My family is going on __________.

5. My family just bought a __________ car.

6. I went shopping for new __________ last weekend.

7. I bought a new __________ game.

___________________ ___________ ___________________
Name   Date   Helper

Questioning in Conversation – Word Search

Instructions: Read each statement and find the <u>underlined</u> word in the puzzle. Then choose five sentences and ask three questions about each one.

```
R  C  V  Z  D  V  O  N  V  M  G  C  V
O  E  A  T  M  R  Y  N  Q  O  N  C  A
J  I  U  H  N  C  V  L  X  V  I  O  S
E  T  A  R  B  E  L  E  C  I  P  J  T
M  T  Y  S  U  B  D  M  I  E  P  X  L
Z  A  I  P  K  B  X  I  J  I  O  B  Z
A  V  S  I  Y  O  M  A  C  N  H  L  K
M  E  K  C  U  A  O  N  A  C  S  V  C
T  O  I  Q  R  H  D  B  W  D  A  M  R
H  H  V  G  C  O  S  T  U  M  E  Y  O
C  O  O  I  I  J  A  Y  E  A  Q  O  Z
R  R  T  F  N  J  A  R  Z  Q  Q  W  P
P  N  U  U  P  G  O  E  D  I  V  I  K
```

1. I saw a great <u>movie</u> last night.

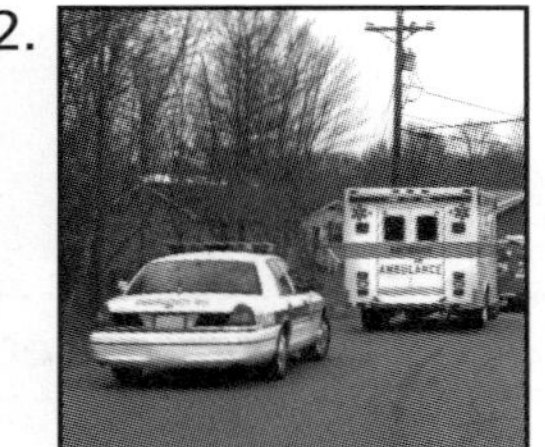

2. There was an <u>accident</u> in my neighborhood.

3. I am <u>moving</u> away.

4. I'm joining a new after-school <u>program</u>.

5. I read some great <u>books</u> this summer.

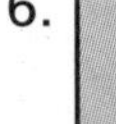

6. We're going out to <u>celebrate</u> tonight.

7. I went <u>shopping</u> for new clothes last weekend.

8. My teacher was <u>upset</u> with the class today.

9. I bought a new <u>video</u> game.

10. I finished my Halloween <u>costume</u>.

Name _______________ Date _______________ Helper _______________

Questioning in Conversation – Draw a Picture

Instructions: Read each statement and draw a picture in the box that goes with it. Ask three questions about each statement.

1.

There's a new mall opening in town today.

4.

Let's go to the beach.

2.

Today, the school bus broke down.

5.

I saw a police officer in front of the bank.

3.

I broke my arm.

6.

My family is going on vacation.

Name   Date   Helper

Questioning in Conversation – Five Word Association

Instructions: Write five words that are associated with each photo. Then ask a question using each word.

A. 

1. _______________________
2. _______________________
3. _______________________
4. _______________________
5. _______________________

B. 

1. _______________________
2. _______________________
3. _______________________
4. _______________________
5. _______________________

C. 

1. _______________________
2. _______________________
3. _______________________
4. _______________________
5. _______________________

D. 

1. _______________________
2. _______________________
3. _______________________
4. _______________________
5. _______________________

E. 

1. _______________________
2. _______________________
3. _______________________
4. _______________________
5. _______________________

F. 

1. _______________________
2. _______________________
3. _______________________
4. _______________________
5. _______________________

G. 

1. _______________________
2. _______________________
3. _______________________
4. _______________________
5. _______________________

H. 

1. _______________________
2. _______________________
3. _______________________
4. _______________________
5. _______________________

I. 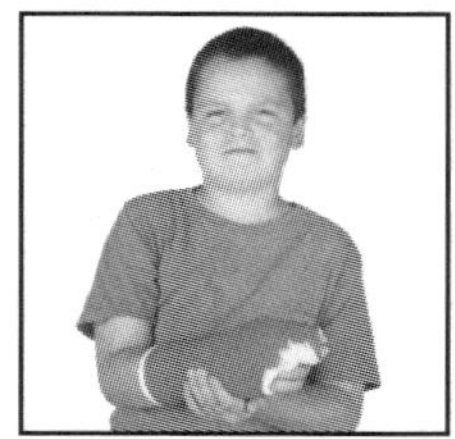

1. _______________________
2. _______________________
3. _______________________
4. _______________________
5. _______________________

_________________________ _________________ _________________
Name   Date   Helper

Questioning in Conversation – Fill It In

Instructions: Look at the photos. Then fill in the blanks with words from the Word Bank to complete the statements. Choose four of the statements, and ask three questions about each one.

─── **Word Bank** ───

teacher	school	closing	accident	concert
tickets	neighborhood	reward	detention	project

1.  I didn't go to

   ____

   yesterday.

2.  I finished my science

   __________________ .

3.  I have

   __________________ .

4.  I received a $100

   __________________ .

5.  They are

   ____

   the park early.

6. 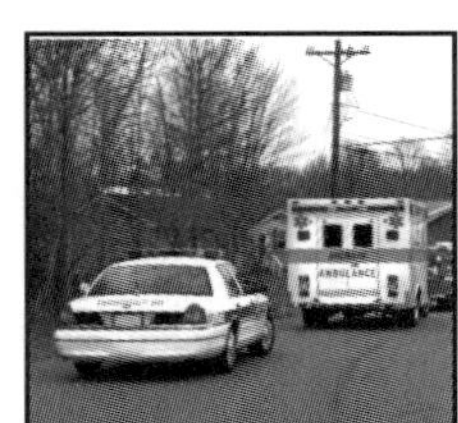 There was an

   ____

   in my

   __________________ .

7.  The __________________

   needs some helpers today.

8.  My mom ordered

   ____

   online for the

   __________________ .

___________________ ___________ ___________
Name Date Helper

Questioning in Conversation – Write a Question

Instructions: Look at each photo and the statement that goes with it. Ask a question about the statement and write it on the lines.

1. There is going to be an assembly in school tomorrow.

2. I am moving away.

3. My teacher was upset with the class today.

4. I read some great books this summer.

5. I finished my Halloween costume.

Name   Date   Helper

Questioning in Conversation – Guess the Statement

Instructions: Look at the photos and read the three questions asked. Can you guess the statement? Write the statement on the line.

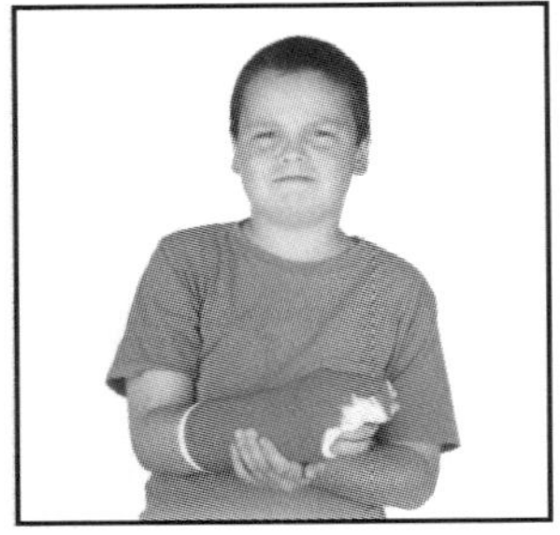

1. Statement: ____

    How did you break your arm?

    How long do you have to wear the cast?

    Does it hurt?

2. Statement: ____

    How long has he been gone?

    Where did you last see him?

    Is there a reward?

3. Statement: ____

    Where did it break down?

    How did you get to school?

    What was wrong with the bus?

4. Statement: ____

    Where are you going?

    How long will you be gone?

    Are you driving or flying?

5. Statement: ____

    Were you sick?

    What did you do all day?

    Do you have any work to make up?

_________________________ _________________ _________________

Name   Date   Helper

Questioning in Conversation – Decode the Word

Instructions: Fill in each blank with the correct word. For help, use the Word Bank. Then transfer each letter that has a number under it to reveal the *Secret Word*. Ask three questions about each statement.

Word Bank

science   teacher   officer
movie   grandmother

1.

I saw a great

_ _ _ _ _ _
  ⑤ ①

last night.

2.

I'm going to visit my

_ _ _ _ _ _ _ _ _ _ _ _ .
      ④   ⑦

3.

I finished my _ _ _ _ _ _ _ project.
              ⑥

4.

The _ _ _ _ _ _ _
      ②

needs some helpers after class.

5.

I saw a police

_ _ _ _ _ _ _
            ③

in front of the bank.

What state is this?

_ _ _ _ _ _ _
1 2 3 4 5 6 7
Secret Word

Name   Date   Helper

Questioning in Conversation – Right or Wrong Question?

Instructions: Read each statement. If the question below is related to the statement, color the *happy* face. If the question is not related to the statement, color the *sad* face. For every sad face you color, ask a question that is related.

1. I received a $100 reward.

   What did you do to get a reward?

2. They are closing the park early.

   Do you like to play on the slide?

3. There is going to be a surprise party for Mary.

   Is it her birthday?

4. Let's go to the beach.

   When are we leaving?

5. My mom ordered tickets online for the concert.

   Did you see the news last night?

6. I have detention.

   Are you going to the movies tonight?

7. Our family just bought a new car.

   What kind did you buy?

8. There's a new mall opening in town today.

   Did you see Mr. Jones in town?

_______________________   _______________   _______________________
Name   Date   Helper

Questioning in Conversation – Be a Detective

Instructions: Look at the photos and statements. Then write three questions you might ask in each situation.

1. I finished my Halloween costume.

   Question 1: ____

   ____

   Question 2: ____

   ____

   Question 3: ____

   ____

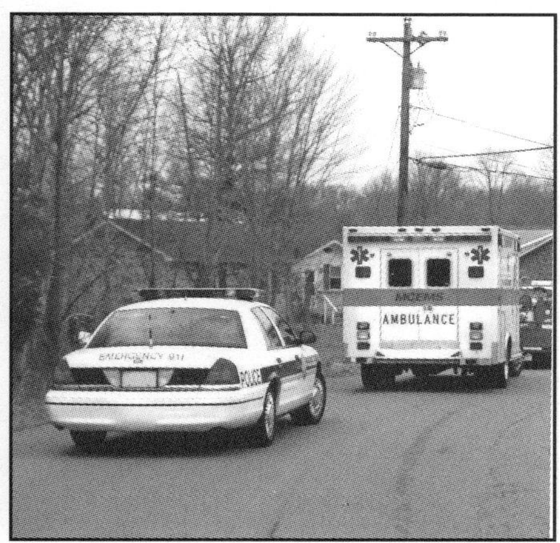

2. There was an accident in my neighborhood.

   Question 1: ____

   ____

   Question 2: ____

   ____

   Question 3: ____

   ____

3. We're going out to celebrate tonight.

   Question 1: ____

   ____

   Question 2: ____

   ____

   Question 3: ____

   ____

______________________   ______________   ______________
Name   Date   Helper

Questioning in Conversation – Asking Why Questions

Instructions: Look at the photos and the statements that go with them. Then write a *Why* question about each one. Ask another related question aloud.

1. I received a $100 reward.

   Why: ____

   ____

2. The teacher needs some helpers after class.

   Why: ____

   ____

3. They are closing the park early.

   Why: ____

   ____

4. I have detention.

   Why: ____

   ____

5. I didn't go to school yesterday.

   Why: ____

   ____

___________________________ _______________ ___________________________
Name   Date   Helper

Answer Key

Page 1
A. 4
B. 3
C. 1
D. 5
E. 2
F. 7
G. 8
H. 6

Page 3
1. Chicago
2. Cape Canaveral
3. Seattle
4. New York City
5. Atlanta
6. Denver
7. Boise
8. Phoenix

Page 4
1. A
2. B
3. C
4. B
5. C

Page 6
1. eagle through binoculars
2. bottle of medicine
3. family under umbrella
4. girl with backpack
5. American flag
6. hikers with compass

Page 8

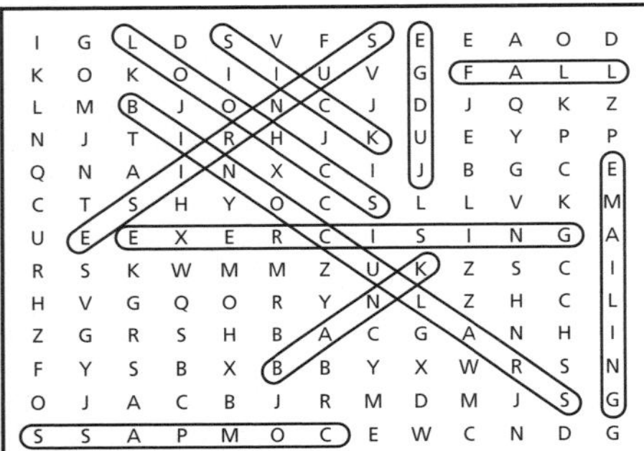

Page 9

Page 12
1. boiling, stove
2. dribble, shot
3. medicine, bed
4. ball, hole
5. scientist, eyepiece
6.
7. sun, sky
8. read, prize
9. lost, needle

Page 15
1. basketball
2. marbles
3. umbrella
4. leaves
5. backpack
Secret Word: Alabama

Page 16
1. happy
2. happy
3. sad
4. sad
5. happy
6. sad
7. happy
8. sad

Determining Perspective

Page 21
1. 3
2. 6
3. 1
4. 4
5. 5
6. 2
7. 7
8. 8

Page 23
1. Rapid City
2. Salt Lake City
3. San Francisco
4. Houston
5. Nashville
6. Miami
7. Boston
8. Minneapolis

Page 24
1. B
2. B
3. A
4. C
5. A

Page 26
1. boy on bleachers
2. boy getting haircut
3. boy at dinner table
4. two swimmers
5. woman receiving gift
6. girl with trophy

Page 29

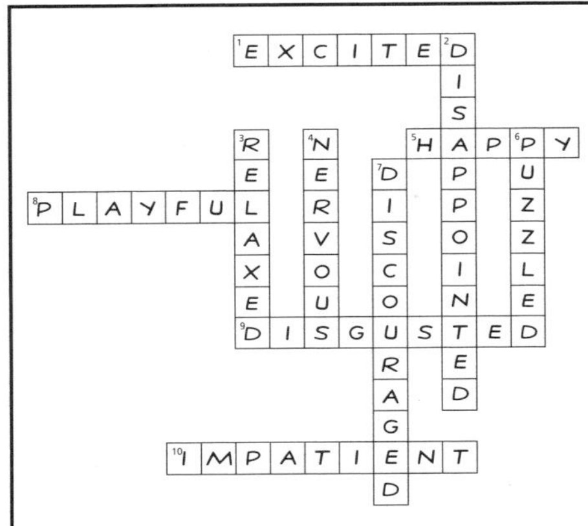

Page 30
1. This old car always breaks down.
2. I hope she brings my drink next.
3. I'm going to be late again.
4. I think my arm is broken.
5. Those golf lessons paid off.

Page 33
1. virus, computer
2. sideburns, short
3. waves, high
4. playing, autumn
5. sushi, disgusting
6. friends, deserted
7. multiplication, math
8. beautiful, bouquet

Page 36
1. fight
2. haircut
3. multiplication
4. abacus
5. binoculars
Secret Word: Missouri

Page 37
1. sad
2. happy
3. happy
4. sad
5. happy
6. sad
7. happy
8. happy

Stating Opinions

Page 41
1. 2
2. 7
3. 4
4. 8
5. 5
6. 1
7. 3
8. 6

Page 43
1. Memphis
2. Las Vegas
3. San Diego
4. Des Moines
5. Sacramento
6. Dallas
7. New Orleans
8. Washington, D.C.

Page 49

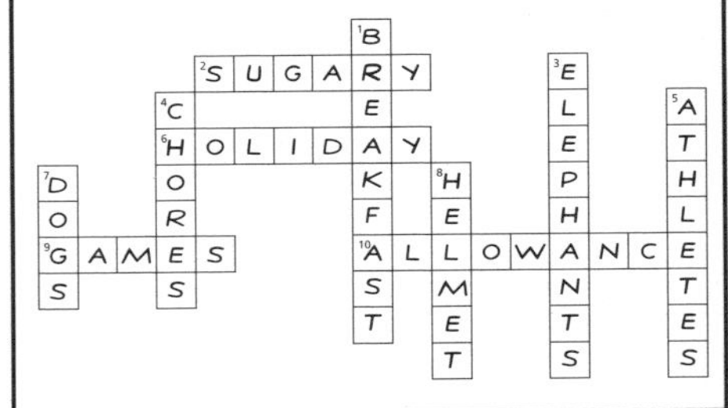

Page 50

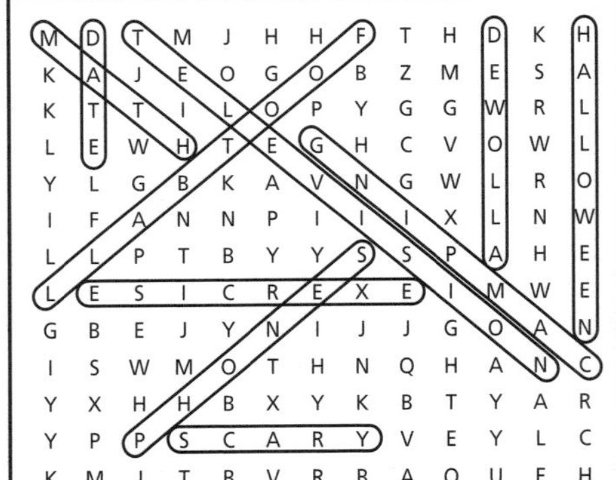

Page 52
1. fact
2. opinion
3. opinion
4. fact
5. fact
6. opinion
7. fact
8. opinion
9. opinion
10. fact

Page 53
1. students, cards
2. watch, program
3. years, babysitter
4. hours, every
5. date, old
6. healthy, candy
7. movies, fun
8. allowed, parks

Page 56

1. holiday
2. elephants
3. breakfast
4. Halloween
5. color

Secret Word: New York

Page 58

1. yellow
2. yellow
3. yellow
4. red
5. red
6. red
7. red
8. red
9. red
10. yellow
11. yellow
12. red
13. red

Intonation & Body Language

Page 61

A. 5
B. 4
C. 2
D. 3
E. 1
F. 8
G. 7
H. 6

Page 63

1. Charlotte
2. Los Angeles
3. Albuquerque
4. Detroit
5. Jacksonville
6. Virginia Beach
7. Austin
8. Rock Springs

Page 64

1. B
2. C
3. A
4. B
5. C

Page 66

1. dollar bill
2. soccer players
3. stack of mail
4. snow-covered bus
5. angry woman
6. sad woman

Page 69

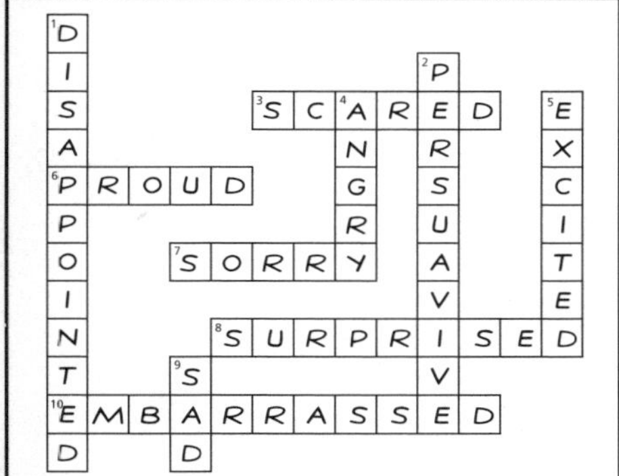

Page 70

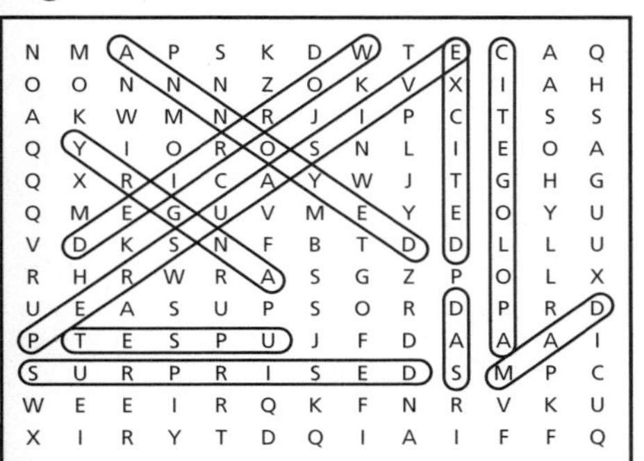

Page 73

1. friend, sad
2. video, frustrated
3. movies, surprised
4. cafeteria, embarrassed
5. birthday, disappointed
6. bear, scared
7. star, excited
8. parents, happy

Page 76

1. upset
2. disappointed
3. embarrassed
4. angry
5. excited

Secret Word: Maine

Page 77

1. happy
2. sad
3. happy
4. sad
5. happy
6. sad
7. sad
8. happy

Social Encouragement

Page 81

A. 5
B. 3
C. 6
D. 8
E. 4
F. 1
G. 7
H. 2

Page 83

1. Las Vegas
2. Memphis
3. Washington, D.C.
4. Des Moines
5. Dallas
6. New Orleans
7. Sacramento
8. San Diego

Page 84

1. B
2. A
3. C
4. B
5. A

Page 86

1. frustrated boy
2. boy with black eye
3. little boy crying
4. teacher with pencil
5. dad paying bills
6. boy in dugout

Page 90

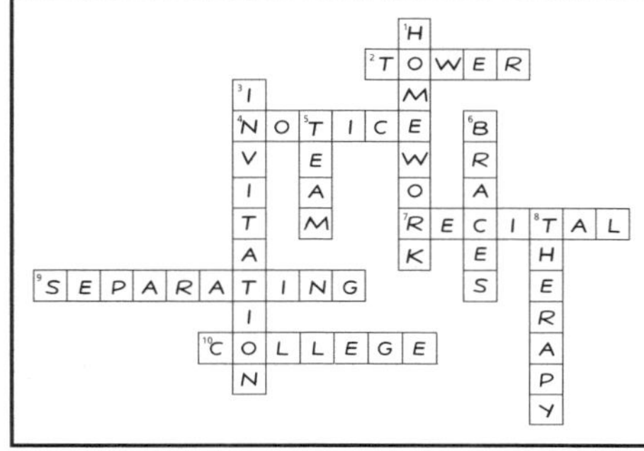

Page 91

1. We can do our homework together.
2. I'll help you build a tower.
3. I'll take you to your classroom.
4. Let's make some lost dog signs.
5. I'll load the dishwasher for you.

Page 94

1. lost, find
2. ruined, dress
3. student, hallway
4. list, feelings
5. upset, failed
6. basket, team
7. curls, picture
8. sleepover, couch

Page 97

1. frustrated
2. worried
3. lonely
4. sad
5. discouraged

Secret Word: Florida

Page 98

1. happy
2. sad
3. sad
4. happy
5. sad
6. happy
7. happy
8. sad

Understanding Sarcasm

Page 101

A. 4
B. 2
C. 7
D. 3
E. 6
F. 8
G. 1
H. 5

Page 103

1. Memphis
2. Las Vegas
3. San Diego
4. Des Moines
5. Dallas
6. Washington, D.C.
7. New Orleans
8. Sacramento

Page 104

1. B
2. C
3. A
4. B
5. A

Page 110

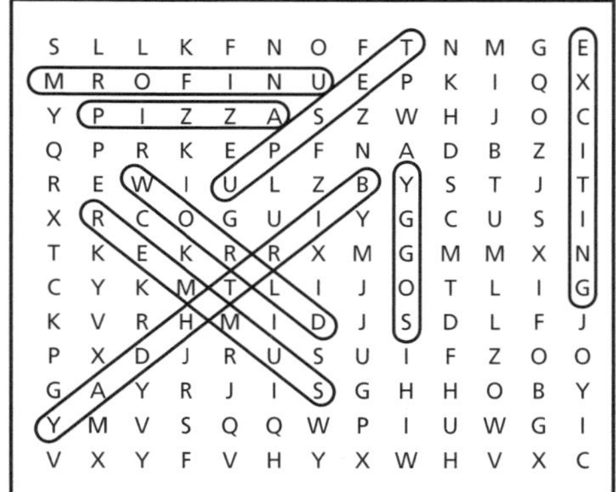

Page 111

1. B
2. D
3. E
4. C
5. A

Page 113

1. brother, camper
2. favorite, love
3. mailbox, mailman
4. costume, clown
5. team, baseball
6. cranky, house
7. tripped, way
8. skiing, again

Continued

Page 116
1. worst
2. hate
3. easy
4. boring
5. funniest
Secret Word:
Ohio

Page 117
1. happy
2. sad
3. sad
4. happy
5. happy
6. sad
7. sad
8. sad

Staying Calm

Page 121
A. 4
B. 6
C. 3
D. 8
E. 5
F. 2
G. 7
H. 1

Page 123
1. Austin
2. Los Angeles
3. Charlotte
4. Jacksonville
5. Detroit
6. Albuquerque
7. Virginia Beach
8. Rock Springs

Page 124
1. C
2. B
3. B
4. A
5. C

Page 126
1. girl on bus
2. boys pointing and laughing
3. boy looking at video game
4. girl pitching
5. boy with face in hands
6. dad and son arguing

Page 129

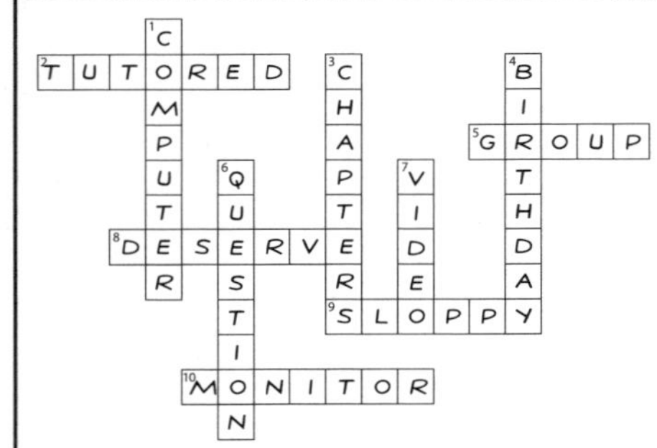

Page 130
1. Oh well, my hair grows fast.
2. Staying focused will help me remember.
3. I can always start my own club.
4. Everyone makes mistakes sometimes.
5. I know it was an accident.

Page 131

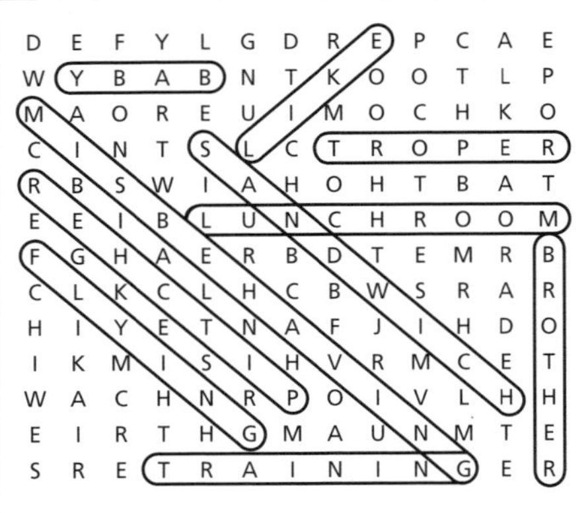

Page 133
1. helper, best
2. brother, late
3. wrong, lunch
4. behind, back
5. Bahamas, afraid
6. baby, bus
7. math, studying
8. championship, training

Page 136
1. first
2. deliver
3. class
4. birthday
5. stop
Secret Word:
Idaho

Page 137
1. happy
2. happy
3. sad
4. sad
5. happy
6. sad
7. sad
8. sad

Predicting

Page 141
A. 3
B. 1
C. 8
D. 5
E. 4
F. 7
G. 2
H. 6

Page 143
1. Memphis
2. Sacramento
3. Dallas
4. San Diego
5. New Orleans
6. Las Vegas
7. Des Moines
8. Washington, D.C.

Page 144
1. B
2. A
3. C
4. A
5. B

Page 146
1. boy texting
2. nails
3. boy eating chips
4. boy studying
5. boy climbing tree
6. freezer

Page 149

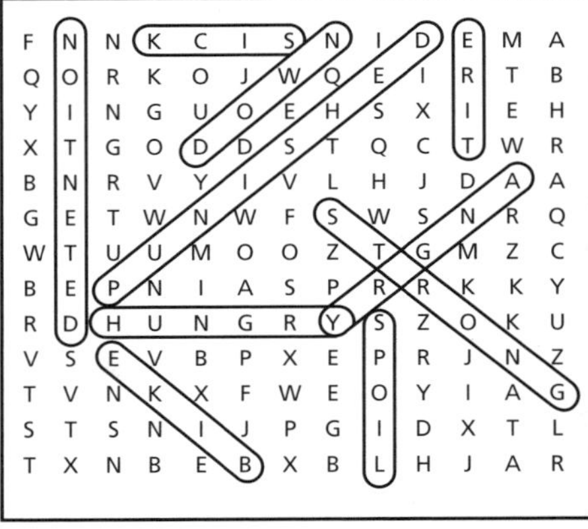

Page 150

Page 153
1. wallet, reward
2. freezer, thaw
3. practice, improve
4. sneaking, punished
5. exercise, strong
6. citizenship, certificate
7. permission, angry
8. volunteer, helpful

Page 156
1. angry
2. hungry
3. outside
4. reward
5. trouble
Secret Word:
Oregon

Page 157
1. happy
2. sad
3. sad
4. happy
5. sad
6. happy
7. happy
8. sad

Cognitive Flexibility

Page 161
A. 3
B. 8
C. 5
D. 2
E. 4
F. 6
G. 1
H. 7

Page 163
1. Albuquerque
2. Detroit
3. Los Angeles
4. Rock Springs
5. Virginia Beach
6. Charlotte
7. Austin
8. Jacksonville

Page 164
1. B, C
2. A, B
3. A, C
4. A, B
5. A, C

Page 166
1. broken window
2. hands with money
3. open window
4. empty plate
5. girl pointing
6. scissors

Page 170
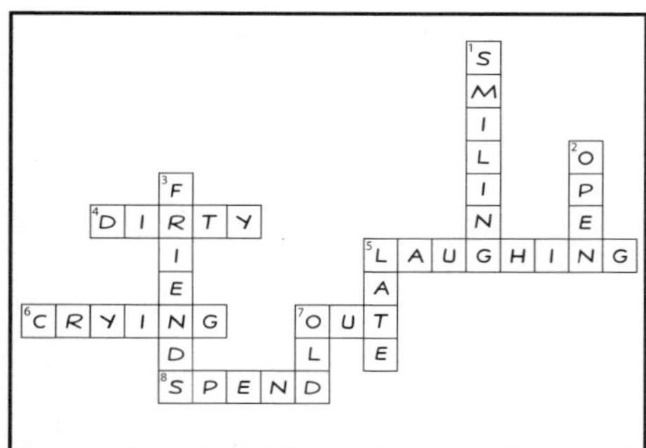

Page 171
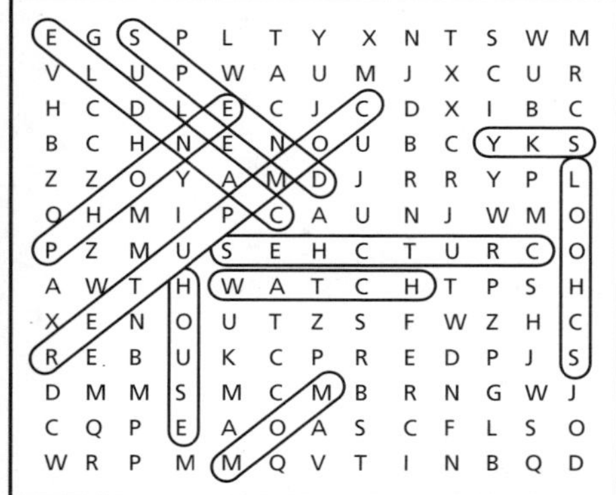

Page 172
1. Why is Emily lighting a candle?
2. Why is Sam walking with crutches?
3. Why is school out today?
4. Why are your old toys missing?
5. Why did you spend $5.00 today?

Page 173
1. car, street
2. computer, working
3. garbage, yard
4. table, gone
5. dad, suitcases
6. wear, clothes
7. attention, please
8. watch, no

Page 176
1. announcement
2. raccoon
3. doctor
4. vacation
5. sick
Secret Word: Nevada

Page 177
1. happy
2. happy
3. sad
4. happy
5. happy
6. sad
7. sad
8. happy

Page 180
1. E
2. D
3. A
4. B
5. C

Questioning in Conversation

Page 181
A. 4
B. 1
C. 6
D. 8
E. 2
F. 7
G. 3
H. 5

Page 183
1. San Diego
2. Sacramento
3. Des Moines
4. Washington, D.C.
5. Las Vegas
6. Dallas
7. New Orleans
8. Memphis

Page 184
1. B
2. C
3. A
4. B
5. A

Page 186
1. school auditorium
2. girl holding up clothes
3. boy with broken arm
4. couple in formal clothes
5. teacher at chalkboard
6. city park

Page 189
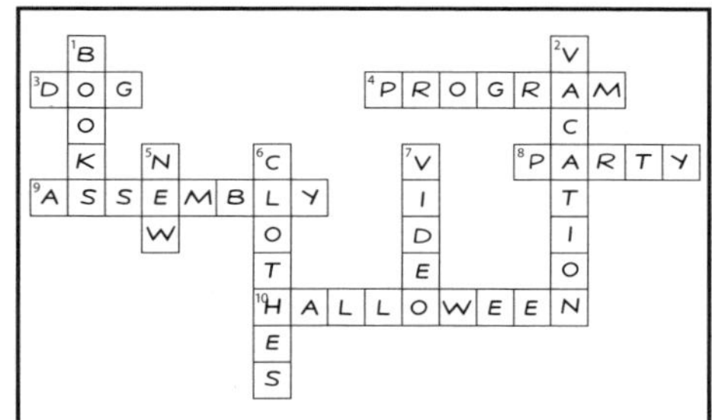

Page 190
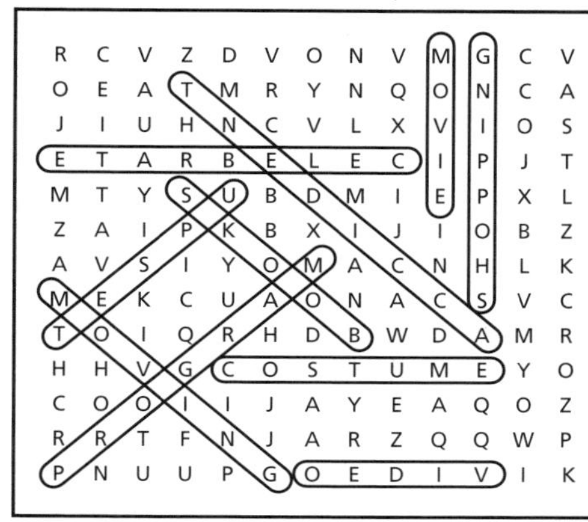

Page 193
1. school
2. project
3. detention
4. reward
5. closing
6. accident, neighborhood
7. teacher
8. tickets, concert

Page 195
1. I broke my arm.
2. My dog ran away.
3. The school bus broke down.
4. My family is going on vacation.
5. I didn't go to school yesterday.

Page 196
1. movie
2. grandmother
3. science
4. teacher
5. officer
Secret Word: Vermont

Page 197
1. happy
2. sad
3. happy
4. happy
5. sad
6. sad
7. happy
8. sad

Congratulations
for your good work!
Student's Name
Date
Speech-Language Pathologist

Excellent!

___________________ HAS
Student's Name

DONE AN

EXCELLENT JOB.

___________________   ___________________
Date   Speech-Language Pathologist

Good Understanding!

Student's Name

completed the task!

____
Date

____
Speech-Language Pathologist

Great Answers!

We honor __________________ for answering all _______ questions correctly.

Student's Name

____

Date

____

Speech-Language Pathologist

Notes